AF553795

GENERAL SECONDARY EDUCATION IN THE 21st CENTURY

Editor

Dr. Digumarti Bhaskara Rao

M.Sc., M.A., M.A., M.Ed., Ph.D.

Reader

R.V.R. College of Education

Srinivasa Nagar Colony

Guntur–522 006

Andhra Pradesh

India

DISCOVERY PUBLISHING HOUSE

NEW DELHI-110002

First Published - 2004
Reprinted - 2016

ISBN: 978-81-7141-885-5

General Secondary Education in the 21st Century

Published by:
DISCOVERY PUBLISHING HOUSE PVT. LTD.
4383/4B, Ansari Road, Darya Ganj
New Delhi-110 002 (India)
Phone: +91-11-23279245, 43596064-65
Fax: +91-11-23253475
E-mail: discoverypublishinghouse@gmail.com
sales@discoverypublishinggroup.com
web: www.discoverypublishinggroup.com

Printed at:
Infinity Imaging Systems
Delhi

Dedicated

To

My Affectionate Classmate And Beloved Friend

Mr. Narne Siva Ram Prasad

And To His Wife

Mrs. Vijaya Lakshmi

—D.B. Rao

"Men often become what they believe themselves to be. If I believe I cannot do some thing, it makes me incapable of doing it. But when I believe I can, then I acquire the ability to do it even if I didn't have it in the beginning."

Mahatma Gandhi
The Father of India

Mulford argued that the above analysis makes it clear that the objectives and functions of Secondary Education do need to be redefined in the twenty-first century. Even if by following the directions pointed to by the compass allows for individual and local ingenuity, the general direction is clearly one indicating a need for reform. However, successful reform will require us to resolve a number of major issues or dilemmas including the balance of general and vocational education, mass and selective schooling and cognitive and behavioural outcomes. These dilemmas are developed in the later sections of this report.

Mulford made one important concluding point—we need to ask what should the future be like in the twenty first century as well as what will the future be like. Education needs something other than the metaphors of decay, disaster and erosion as driving forces of change. As Leclercq's (2001) working document for the meeting pointed out, "the analysis of context cannot merely consist in identifying overwhelming trends to which we must necessarily submit. Among those trends, we have to differentiate between what is acceptable and what is not". Children are the starting point for a strategy about the future of schooling. A constructive and optimistic vision of their futures and needs should inform the structure and processes of education.

2. COUNTRY PAPERS, PRESENTATIONS, DISCUSSION AND DEBATE

As Leclercq's (2001) working document for the meeting pointed out, General Secondary Education "is no longer reserved, as in the past, for the minority of the most fortunate youth. Nor is it any longer the prime of secondary education to afford access to higher studies, even if that remains very much a goal...preparation for working life has become as important in secondary education as preparation for higher studies".

Leclercq (2001) maintained that societal change and the increased demand for Secondary Education will result in changes in curricula, teaching methods and school operations. "First and foremost, the syllabus needs to be modernised...disciplines...must be upgraded. Room has also to

Preface

Secondary education is a crucial point in the lives of individuals; it is at this stage that young people should be able to decide their own future, in the light of their own tastes and aptitudes, and that they can acquire the abilities that will make for a successful adult life. (Delor's Report). Aware of the fundamental importance of education and the growing need to focus on secondary education, the international community has taken up the challenge of improving the relevance and effectiveness of secondary education.

In order to complement international efforts and facilitate policy dialogue on this commitment to secondary education, the UNESCO International Expert Meeting on General Secretary Education in the Twenty-First Century: Trends, Challenges and Priorities was held in Beijing, China. The report of the meeting is presented in this book along with some important papers on the theme. This book also contains the results of the UNESCO's International Conference on the Reform of Secondary Education held in Muscat, Sultanate of Oman. All these conclusions and suggestions are specifically meant for the quality improvement of secondary education around the world.

This book will be useful to educational planners and policy makers, educational personnel, and teachers and students in the light of the globalisation of human resource development as this book is specially prepared for their use.

I am very much thankful to Dr. (Mrs.) Sonia Bahri, Chief of the Section for General Secondary Education, UNESCO, Paris for immediately sending and granting permission for reproduction of the material that reproduced in this book upon my request. I am thankful to the UNESCO, Paris and to the Ministry of Education, Sultanate of Oman, Muscat for reproducing the material from their publications in order to disseminate the information on secondary education among the people and personnel involved in the area of secondary education. Thanks are also to all the authors— Prof. Bill Mulford, Dr. Sonia Bahri, Prof. Jean–Michel Leclercq and others who made this publication possible.

Dr. Digumarti Bhaskara Rao

Research Director in Education

Nagarjuna University

br_digumarti@rediffmail.com

Contents

adequate resources. However, selection can occur not only to, but also in, Secondary Education. In order to overcome the disadvantage inherent in this situation, Mr. Wright argued for a move from a sellers' to a buyers' market.

- Access to Secondary Education involves both issues of provision and uptake. Provision does not guarantee uptake. Barriers to initial access, persistence and completion include school-related barriers, home or community related barriers and wider societal barriers. What is needed are access conditions that encourage all to participate, legislation that discourages school refusal, no pedagogical impediments, socio-economic conditions that stimulate participation, and a political ideology and orientation favouring participation.
- Mass education can accentuate disadvantages. This is the irony of mass education without universal education where an isolated few without access raise the persistent issue of equity. There is clearly a need to move beyond mass education to universal education. But universal access to Secondary Education raises other issues including resourcing, alternative provisions and delivery mechanisms, and the ability to liberalise laws governing provision especially to eliminate gender disparities.
- Selection as a rationing mechanism to Secondary Education has included selective entrance examinations and a hierarchy of school types for entrance. Such mechanisms usually compound privileges in the name of merit. Selection can also occur within universal Secondary Education through the structure of the curriculum (academic/vocational), streaming and access to streams, the options and choices available, and student choices and consequences of such choices.

Mr. Wright argued that it was time to consider empowering learners as selectors. It was time to move from a seller's market

1

Introduction

The Dakar Framework for Action (UNESCO, 2000) states that "Education is a fundamental human right. It is the key to sustainable development and peace and stability within and among countries, and thus an indispensable means for effective participation in the societies and economies of the twenty-first century, which are affected by rapid globalisation".

More specifically, the Delors Report exhorts us to see Secondary Education "as a crucial point in the lives of individuals: it is at this stage that young people should be able to decide their own future, in the light of their own tastes and aptitudes, and that they can acquire the abilities that will make for a successful adult life". The report continues that Secondary Education, "should thus be adapted to take account both of the different processes whereby adolescents attain maturity...and of economic and social needs".

Aware of the fundamental importance of education and the growing need to focus on Secondary Education, the international community has taken up the challenge. Clear commitments have been made within the Dakar framework for action to improve the relevance and effectiveness of Secondary Education. Included in these commitments is agreement to eliminate gender disparities in secondary education by 2005 and achieve gender equality in education by 2015. The focus will be on ensuring girls full and equal access to and achievement in education of good quality.

In order to complement international efforts and facilitate policy dialogue on this commitment to Secondary Education, as well as to learn more about new developments occurring at field-level, the UNESCO International Expert Meeting on General Secondary Education in the Twenty-First Century: Trends, Challenges and Priorities was held in Beijing, People's Republic of China, from 21 to 25 May, 2001. In attendance at this meeting were:

- high level officials responsible within Ministries for Secondary Education from eight countries in different regions and varying contexts, from the least developed and most highly populated countries to the developing and developed nations, balanced in terms of gender, namely, Australia, Bangladesh, Canada, the People's Republic of China, Republic of Guinea, Lebanon, Mexico, and the Russian Federation;
- two international experts in the field of Secondary Education reform;
- a number of experts and other invited observers from the People's Republic of China;
- staff from the National Commission of the People's Republic of China for UNESCO;
- staff from UNESCO Beijing and Paris including the Director of Secondary, Technical and Vocational Education and Chief of the Section for General Secondary Education;
- a rapporteur.

2

The Meeting: Opening, Aims and Organisation

Ms. Shi Shuyan, Deputy Secretary-General, National Commission of the People's Republic of China for UNESCO, welcomed participants and then Mr. Qian Tang, Director of Secondary, Technical and Vocational Education and Chief of the Section for General Secondary Education, reminded participants of the existing international agreements on education, including education for all by 2015 and elimination of gender differences by 2005. Mr. Tang then sought the meetings' view on the importance that should be given to Secondary Education and, if it was of high importance, the advice that could be given to UNESCO in terms priorities for action.

Ms. Sonia Bahri, Chief of the Section, detailed the three specific aims of the meeting for General Secondary Education as:

- to identify the contexts and educational trends facing us now and in the future and the implications of these contexts and trends for the objectives and functions of Secondary Education;
- to identify the challenges and dilemmas arising from this analysis of the contexts and trends;
- to identify priority areas, the resources and strategies required to respond to the objectives and manage the dilemmas.

The agenda for and this final report of the Beijing International Expert Meeting were organised around these three aims. For the first two aims, summaries are provided of the expert background paper, country papers and presentations, discussion and debate, and conclusions reached by the meeting. Also reported are the results of an opportunity for participants to identify areas of non-government as well as other challenges. For the third aim, a summary is made of country papers and presentations, discussion and debate and a list is provided of participants' agreements and advice. A concluding section summarises these agreements and advice in the context of the Dakar Framework.

3

The Context: Do the Objectives and Functions of Secondary Education Need to be Redefined in the Twenty-first Century?

1. BACKGROUND DOCUMENT

In his background document Professor Bill Mulford argued that at the beginning of the twenty-first century it is only right that we take stock of the many changes in the world around us and to affirm the purposes of the education we are providing and that a broad-brush approach to this stock-taking is most helpful—for when lost on a highway a road map is useful but when lost in a swamp, whose topography is constantly changing, a compass which indicates the general direction and allows individual and local ingenuity is better. Mulford identified four compass points, four major dimensions of change in the social context, as well as some of the implications of each for education. The four dimensions were the new conditions for learning (N), the society (S), the economy (E), and the workplace (W).

Society

- Given societal pressures from increased connectedness, greater complexity, uncertainty and diversity, and continued deprivations, including the fact that many young people are themselves on the margins of society rather than playing a constructive role, successful educational provision clearly faces high demands on human factors and social interaction in a knowledge society.

- Education in the twenty-first century needs to focus more on:
  - ❑ In addition to cognitive outcomes, the non-cognitive, behavioural aspects of education, including social competency and learning;
  - ❑ People who can more from one body of knowledge to another and from one set of skills to another with relative ease—what is important is not how much a person has learnt, but how much they are capable of learning and how much knowledge they create over their life-time;
  - ❑ People with critical, creative and flexible communicative competence (especially for an era of global communisations and 'hard sell');
  - ❑ Youth being enlisted in the task of sustainable development—young people are of necessity the future society and their commitment to its development in a constructive way is crucial.
- Good schools model such focuses and are seen as social communities rather than as places of mere academic study. Good schools are also closely associated with the development of the social capital of their community including both genders.

Economy

- Societies are moving away from an industrial economy and towards a knowledge economy. The scope for unskilled labour is shrinking. There is an increase in the proportion of the labour force that is part-time or casual in small and medium size enterprises and self-employment. There is a decrease in repetitive and routine work and increased workplace reliance on skills, adaptability and problem-solving skills. The challenge of these changes in the economy and its labour force to education is great.

- The entire concept of the current education system that mirrors the time in which it developed, a time dominated by government-regulated endeavours in an industrial society with its industrial manufacturing processes, is questioned. In a way, students in the current system are regarded as raw material and processed en masse in places called schools. Students are constantly scrutinised by quality control mechanisms, such that some are selected for further processing and refinement, many others are rejected as 'wastage' or second-class products.
- Even for those who 'succeed', it is suggested that changes in the nature of the labour market have made completion of secondary education and passing achievement tests largely useless credentials for labour market purposes—that is, either for successful individual employment or for a more productive workforce for the economy.
- The new objectives of education in the twenty-first century need to focus more on:
    - ❑ Learning rather than a tightly prescribed, controlled and examined knowledge qualification;
    - ❑ Initiative or entrepreneurship;
    - ❑ Behavioural outcomes including life-skills.
- Despite an increasing recognition that in knowledge-based societies and economies countries neglect their education system at their economic peril, another recent response to changes in national economies has been for some governments to seek to reduce public expenditure, including that to education. Among other things, this reduced expenditure has resulted in an older teaching force that tends to be resistant to change and a lack of resources to successfully develop and implement the needed changes.

- This situation has in some cases meant an unfortunate and greater involvement by governments in education. Unfortunate because more directives seem to have been issued and time lines for meeting the directives seem to have shrunk to fit the time between elections. Unfortunate because of an increasing obsession to reduce acceptable outcomes to a narrowly defined and readily measurable set of skills and levels of achievement on those skills. Successful redefinition of the objectives and functions of Secondary Education is a much longer-term proposition involving a wide set of outcomes, some of which are not easily measured.

Work

- New work patterns have led directly to higher levels of unemployment, especially for young people—including those with only Primary Education. At the other end of the education scale, employers are saying that a degree is not enough and that many university graduates, do not have the qualities they are looking for, that is the ability to communicate, work in teams, adapt to change, be innovate and creative, and have familiarity with the new technology.
- As well, when individuals are no longer prepared for specific occupations and when they have to face a variety of specialisations in their working lives, it is not meaningful for all to follow the same curriculum with the same expectations. It may also be unrealistic to expect education to prepare the young for work, especially in the sense of specific vocational skills.
- Yet, in the industrial society model of education, students undergo the same teaching with the same curriculum. Students have no control over their own learning path or peace. Many of the failures of such a system are simply those who do not fit the uniform production process. The new objectives of education in the twenty-first century will need to focus more on

collective rather than individual intelligence (Brown and Lauder, 2001) that supports the position that:

- ❑ All are capable rather than a few;
- ❑ Intelligence is multiple rather than a matter of solving puzzles with only one right answer;
- ❑ Imagination and emotional engagement are as important as technical expertise;
- ❑ Our ability to imagine alternative futures and to solve open-ended problems, and our interpersonal skills, be included in our definition of intelligence;
- ❑ There is a need to acquire new knowledge continuously throughout one's life.

- What can be learnt effectively at school may be the more generic competencies, necessary for all work and applicable to a wide range of circumstances. For example, the Australian State of Queensland's recent educational review (Education Queensland, 2001) resulted in four new basic clusters for organising the curriculum: life pathways and social futures (who am I and where am I going?); multiliteracies and communications media (how do I make sense of and communicate with the world?); active citizenship (what are my rights and responsibilities in communities, cultures and economies?); and environments and technologies (how do I describe, analyse and shape the world around me?).

New Conditions for Learning

- The new conditions for learning resulting from the continual increase in Secondary school enrolments raises the crucial issues of mass and/or selective secondary education as well as the choice that might be needed to be made between a common school for all and a variety of specialised programmes offered by different schools.

- Whatever the choice, preparation for university education is no longer an adequate rationale, especially with so many going from secondary schools to employment, or technical and vocational education, or even to unemployment.
- But, as is implied in the above sections, the heavy flow from Primary into Secondary Education can be seen as the trigger but not the only cause of the need for secondary school reform. Changes in the society, the economy and the work-place all place pressure on Secondary schools to consider new conditions for learning.
- Other pressures on Secondary schools and their conditions for learning include: transitions from dependence to independence among our youth that happened naturally, as part of normal living with the normal institutions, particularly the family and church, are no longer guaranteed; the age of puberty has fallen; marriage and the commencement of child-birth are occurring later; there is less interaction between parents and children; certainty of employment has diminished; and, the growth of youth culture has been accompanied by an emphasis on material consumption.
- Developments in information technology have also changed the interrelationship of individuals and knowledge. Crucial to such change is the ease of access to information without needing anyone else's assistance or permission to use it through affordable computers and the World Wide Web. If information is readily available to individuals through personal means, what then is the role of teachers and the school? Non-formal and distance education certainly becomes more viable. But raw information is not yet useful knowledge. Teachers have the undeniable role of helping students in selecting, analysing and synthesising available information, and facilitating application and creation of knowledge.

- Unfortunately in this transition period between the old and new conditions for learning has been increasing numbers of areas via for inclusion in the curriculum. The curriculum has become overcrowded. The more crowded a curriculum becomes the shallower and more superficial the educational experience becomes, with particularly disastrous effects on the most at-risk learners.

- The new conditions for learning raise the issue of the degree to which another the curriculum can be planned. There are undoubtedly areas of learning that must be planned and must take place sequentially, such as learning mathematics. However, most of our knowledge is not learnt in a planned manner. Learning is no longer seen purely as an activity occurring in isolated brain or body cells but also in social environments—it is by active discovery and exchange that we learn best. Learning through social experience cannot be engineered.

- The new learning conditions imply a clear need for new patterns of operation by secondary schools. Form needs to follow function. Those in and responsible for Secondary schools will need to adopt:

  ❑ New, flexible, facilitative ways of working (both as subject specialists and/or all-round educators);

  ❑ Educational teams open to other than teachers;

  ❑ New democratic, decentralised ways of governing their schools.

- Above all, those in Secondary schools need to model the new conditions for learning—they need to be involved in:

  ❑ a learning organisation or learning community (where teachers are learners, including being learning partners with the students).

Mulford argued that the above analysis makes it clear that the objectives and functions of Secondary Education do need to be redefined in the twenty-first century. Even if by following the directions pointed to by the compass allows for individual and local ingenuity, the general direction is clearly one indicating a need for reform. However, successful reform will require us to resolve a number of major issues or dilemmas including the balance of general and vocational education, mass and selective schooling and cognitive and behavioural outcomes. These dilemmas are developed in the later sections of this report.

Mulford made one important concluding point—we need to ask what should the future be like in the twenty first century as well as what will the future be like. Education needs something other than the metaphors of decay, disaster and erosion as driving forces of change. As Leclercq's (2001) working document for the meeting pointed out, "the analysis of context cannot merely consist in identifying overwhelming trends to which we must necessarily submit. Among those trends, we have to differentiate between what is acceptable and what is not". Children are the starting point for a strategy about the future of schooling. A constructive and optimistic vision of their futures and needs should inform the structure and processes of education.

2. COUNTRY PAPERS, PRESENTATIONS, DISCUSSION AND DEBATE

As Leclercq's (2001) working document for the meeting pointed out, General Secondary Education "is no longer reserved, as in the past, for the minority of the most fortunate youth. Nor is it any longer the prime of secondary education to afford access to higher studies, even if that remains very much a goal...preparation for working life has become as important in secondary education as preparation for higher studies".

Leclercq (2001) maintained that societal change and the increased demand for Secondary Education will result in changes in curricula, teaching methods and school operations. "First and foremost, the syllabus needs to be modernised...disciplines...must be upgraded. Room has also to be made for subjects which have until now been virtually ignored, such as the new information and communication technologies, civics, and inter-cultural education, not to mention increased provision for artistic culture or physically or sporting activities. ... [Changes] in content must be accompanied by changes in teaching methods...it is by active discovery and exchange that we learn. ...We have to now concern ourselves with the whole person and his/her diversity. ...[Changes in curricula and teaching methods call for] the adoption of new ways of working by teachers, ... the formation of educational teams which are open to the entire educational community, ... [and] democratically based rules of conduct ... adopted as far as possible through dialogue and participation".

Country reports, presentations, discussion and debate were all sympathetic to the arguments presented in both the Mulford and Leclercq background papers. For example, the Russian Federation paper (Barannikov, 2001) stated that the "transition to an information society is a great change in civilisation in the contemporary world" and that this and the trends in Russia's development "demand that the goals of school education should be revised". Bangladesh (Huque, 2001) noted that "with the globalisation movement comes the notion of 'global citizens' that necessitates a new form of education" and that "UNESCO's present initiative for assisting Member States in reforming Secondary Education to meet changing needs of the twenty-first century is a unique coincidence with the reform of education in Bangladesh". The Bangladesh Government's plan for 1995-2010 (Huque, 2001) "identifies the general objectives for the post-primary sub-sectors ... [including] the attainment of universal secondary education".

A comment from the Canadian delegate provided a flavour of the required changes when she stated that "the focus needs to be on the individual and life-long learning through discovery. Connections across the curriculum and what are important. Schools should be at the service of students and only a bare bones curriculum is required in order to achieve community flexibility and learner centredness". The Chinese delegation also stressed the importance of students "learning by themselves".

While the demand for education was seen by delegates to be self-feeding—for example, for Mexico (Arancibia 2001) "seven out of ten choose to continue to their secondary studies" —they also agreed with Wright's (2000) concern that no matter how big they get "Education systems which remain very prescriptive and restrictive will become counter productive". Wright (2000) believes that "the desire for continuous learning, as a survival imperative in a rapidly changing world, means that we will have to liberalise the time-bound and place-bound nature of our current education process".

3. CONCLUSIONS

After an extensive and wide-ranging discussion and debate on the background and country papers, consensus was reached that:

- Secondary Education should be given high priority;
- The objectives and functions of Secondary Education need to be redefined for the twenty-first century.

This consensus was strongly reinforced by Mr. Li Lianning, Director General of Basic Education of the Chinese Ministry of Education when he stated, both in his paper on 'Reform of Secondary Education in China' and in his welcoming remarks at the dinner he hosted for meeting participants, that Chinese education was at a cross-roads, at a transition from basic to Secondary Education. He added that because of this transition and the fact that China was soon to hold its first National Education Planning Meeting, the deliberations and recommendations from the meeting would be of great value for his country.

4

The Themes: Major Dilemmas Secondary Education is or Will Be Facing

After agreeing that Secondary Education should be given high priority and that the objectives and functions of Secondary Education need to be redefined for the twenty-first century, the meeting turned its attention to the major dilemmas Secondary Education is, or will be, facing—the balances in mass and selective schooling, general and specialised (vocational) education and cognitive and behavioural and life-skills outcomes. In what follows an outline is provided of the background document, then the country reports and presentations, and discussion and debate and finally any conclusions reached about each of the dilemmas. Also reported are the results of an opportunity for participants to identify areas of non-agreement on the three dilemmas as well as to list other important issues.

1. MASS ACCESS VERSUS SELECTION

Background Document

In his background document Mr. Cream Wright pointed out that mass access involves both provision and uptake but that a number of barriers usually prevent full uptake. While there is a need to more beyond mass to universal education, such a move has its own problems, not the least of which involves adequate resourcing. However, selection can occur not only to, but also in, Secondary Education. In order to overcome the disadvantage inherent in this situation, Mr. Wright argued for a move from a sellers' to a buyers' market.

- Access to Secondary Education involves both issues of provision and uptake. Provision does not guarantee uptake. Barriers to initial access, persistence and completion include school-related barriers, home or community related barriers and wider societal barriers. What is needed are access conditions that encourage all to participate, legislation that discourages school refusal, no pedagogical impediments, socio-economic conditions that stimulate participation, and a political ideology and orientation favouring participation.
- Mass education can accentuates disadvantages. This is the irony of mass education without universal education where an isolated few without access raise the persistent issue of equity. There is clearly a need to move beyond mass education to universal education. But universal access to Secondary Education raises other issues including resourcing, alternative provisions and delivery mechanisms, and the ability to liberalise laws governing provision especially to eliminate gender disparities.
- Selection as a rationing mechanism to Secondary Education has included selective entrance examinations and a hierarchy of school types for entrance. Such mechanisms usually compound privileges in the name of merit. Selection can also occur within universal Secondary Education through the structure of the curriculum (academic/vocational), streaming and access to streams, the options and choices available, and student choices and the consequences of such choices.

Mr. Wright argued that it was time to consider empowering learners as selectors. It was time to move from a seller's market towards a buyers's market. Such a change could result in flexibility and choice for learners, greater use of ICT in alternative provision and much more responsive institutions.

Country Reports, Presentations, Discussion and Debate

Country reports, presentations, discussion and debate tended to support the directions argued for in the background paper. There was strong support from Australia (Smith, 2001) for the move from "the supply to a demand side" in the provision of Secondary Education. The Mexican delegate (Arancibia, 2001) emphasised her country's priority "to expand Secondary Education above all in rural areas, to ethnic populations, and with minorities" and a number of delegates highlighted the importance of having systems in place for alternative access. The Guinean delegate (Kone, 2001) argued forcefully for the system of Secondary Education to have "footbridges of catchup".

A particular concern of delegates focussed on the assessment systems in place in many countries and the need for them to be changed. For example, in Bangladesh (Haque, 2001) "Private spending on secondary and higher education also tends to be wasted on private tuition to prepare for external examinations which emphasise memorisation of facts rather than problem-solving and analytical skills" and "The present terminal examinations...test the wrong things and distort the teaching process towards factual material rather than analytical skills". The Russian delegate (Barannikov, 2001) agreed that the "assessment system should be directed not so much towards establishing the measure of assimilating (remembering) the students' minimum formal-knowledge component but reveal their ability to employ the content they have assimilated in solving practical, cognitive, value-oriented, and communicative tasks and problems".

The Chinese Joint Innovative Project on Raising the Quality of Secondary School Training (Ni Chuanrong, 2001) aimed "at changing exam-oriented education into quality education" by evolving "an evaluation system at three levels comprising student self-assessment, assessment between students and the teacher and teacher assessment". In Australia

(Smith, 2001) the integration and cross fertilisation of general Secondary and Vocational Education and Training has brought advantages to the pedagogy and learning traditions of both areas, especially in the area of assessment and reporting on student learning: "One of the most significant achievements in Australian schooling in recent years has been the development of benchmarks of standard of achievement expected of students at successive stages of education. These benchmarks are the conceptual equivalents of the competencies used to define standards of Vocational Education and Training within the Australian Training Framework. Finding practical ways of relating standards, or criterion based, assessment with competency cased assessment will be a strong clue to support the continuing coming together of General and Vocational Education in Australia".

Discussion centred on the issue of the predictive validity of assessment systems and the fact that examination marks are not necessarily good predictors of either university or later job income success. Unfortunately students who want to pass examinations and teachers who want to keep their jobs may be colluding in the retention of out of date examination systems. Further concern was expressed that examinations distort the curriculum and what is taught and tend to perpetuate privilege. As the Canadian delegate commented, "We need to measure what we value rather than value what we measure".

Conclusions

After an extensive and wide-ranging discussion and debate on the background and country papers and country presentations, consensus was reached that:

- Countries should continue to be committed to the goal of mass secondary education as a minimum in terms of policy and provision.
- Commitment to universal access to Secondary Education as an aspiration should be maintained with efforts to remove barriers and obstacles especially for girls as well as build on strengths and opportunities.

- Serious attention needs to be given to making adequate provision for those not selected into Secondary Education, those who drop out or leave before completing the cycle and those denied access to their preferred streams within the system of mass Secondary Education system.

- Whilst the transition from primary to Secondary and/ or from lower Secondary to upper secondary is not 100 per cent in many countries, efforts must be made to accommodate all those who are eligible through alternative provisions and other measures such as double shift schools and distance education. Where this is not possible available places should be allocated equitably (gender, class, etc.) as well as transparently. (Selection) The criterion for selection in some countries is a "selective examination". In some other cases available places are allocated on a first-come-first-served basis whilst in yet other cases places are allocated on the basis of continuous assessment and/ or annual examination results.

- In many countries mass access to Secondary Education will require partnership between governments and other providers (private, NGOs, etc.), but governments should seek to safeguard the interests of learners by ensuring quality standards are maintained in alternative provisions of Secondary Education. Where there is already a strong tradition of alternative provision (*e.g.* Bangladesh private community schools) governments should build on this by assisting and strengthening these schools.

- Structure of programmes and streaming practices should be reviewed to offer greater flexibility and choice to learners in the selection process including the option to return to a preferred stream.

- Future orientation at Secondary level should be towards greater quality and diversity of what is provided, more flexibility in the organisation of learning and greater responsiveness of Secondary Education institutions to the needs and circumstances of learners. (Empowering learners for selection).

2. GENERAL VERSUS SPECIALISED (VOCATIONAL) EDUCATION

Background Document

In his background document Mr. Cream Wright first identified the reasons for, and the key issues in, the provision of formal education. He then turned to key issues in the provision of general and specialised (vocational) education. He concluded with the two lessons for the future regarding the status of Vocational Education and its place in life-long learning.

Formal education at all levels at is essentially about supply and demand, or more accurately about provision and uptake. What are the reasons for the acquisition of prescribed learning in a formal setting? What is it that motivates citizens to seek opportunities for acquiring certain learning experiences? Answers to these questions have a universal as well as a national and local dimension. The following are some of the elements in answers that can help us to better understand the key issues involved in the general nature of education:

- Every society needs to prepare its citizens for the roles and responsibilities that are essential for that society to function and survive as a recognisable cultural, economic, social and political entity.
- Agencies that have traditionally been responsible for preparing citizens for the various roles in society include the family (nuclear and extended); religious organisations; community-based groups; political parties and interest groups; skilled trades (guides); and the formal school system. What all these agencies do can broadly be labelled "education" or education and training.
- The more developed and complex a society becomes, the more diverse and diffused are the roles and

responsibilities involved, and more formalised becomes the process of education (increasingly) located in a school system).

- Education concerns a wide spectrum of prescribed learning intended to cover the cultural, economic, social and political dimensions of human development. It is through these that society survives, functions and progresses in a dynamic manner. As formal schooling increasingly becomes the sole or main repository for providing education, the structure, content and management of the process of schooling becomes increasingly complex and politicised.

- Most societies do not limit prescribed learning to the functional requirements of current roles and responsibilities (education is not purely utilitarian). There is also a concern with how society relates to other societies, how to achieve a new society as envisioned by those in authority, as well as a concern with the esoteric business of acquiring/pursuing knowledge for its own sake.

- On the demand side, every individual needs to understand his/her place in society and must learn to perform various roles and responsibilities in order to be a functional member of that society. This is a major driving force underlying the broad demand for education on the part of learners.

- Individuals, families and communities are deeply aware that they need a range of knowledge and skills to survive, function and progress within society. They are therefore constantly seeking means by which they can fulfil these needs. It is yet another major driving force behind the demand for education and the search for learning opportunities.

- There is an innate curiosity and desire to learn that is an integral part of human nature and central to the concept of human beings as problem-solving creatures. This is yet another (non-utilitarian) factor underlying the demand for education by individuals and communities.

These answers lead to a number of key issues in the demand, provision and uptake of education.

- Historically the provision of formal education has tended to be dominated by a functional and utilitarian ideology, at least from the supply point of view. Society has tended to provide for education to the extent that this was necessary to meet certain public goals, such as skilled manpower for economic production, human resources for the government machinery, a citizenry that conforms to certain norms of behaviour, the preservation of a heritage and way of life that is highly valued, etc.
- There has also been a competing ideology of education as liberation, which is more to do with the benefits and goals of individuals and communities than with general public goals. In this sense, education is seen as an empowering force that raises consciousness, improves self-reliance and helps individuals and communities to achieve their full development potential.
- More recently there has been an increasing convergence towards the ideology of education as a basic human right. This entails both an obligation on the part of society to ensure appropriate provision of educational opportunities, and a right on the part of individuals and communities to access such provision without undue barriers and obstacles. It is an ideology that is pregnant with implications for political and social bargaining in the area of education.
- Whatever the predominant ideology, education is ultimately about resources. The key issues are to do with use of public resources for providing education, and the role of private resources in accessing such education opportunities.

- A critical issue related to resource, is what these resources (public/private) should be invested in. This concerns levels of education and areas of education, as well as target groups of beneficiaries. Who provides (funds) and who benefits, and what are the choices and options available within this mix?
- It needs to be appreciated that public resources are not limitless and that there are other competing priorities for these resources, apart from the education sector. This is an important caveat on the obligation of governments to provide education under the "rights" ideology. The trend has been towards the use of public resources to guarantee the rights of the disadvantaged, whilst ensuring that choice (based on use of private resources) for less disadvantaged groups is not stifled. This is a complex process fraught with controversy, as it often involves curtailing entrenched privileges enjoyed by groups that are already advantaged in educational as well as economic and political terms.

This analysis raises a number of issues to do with Secondary Education in general and specialised (vocational) education in particular.

- The concept of Secondary Education can be defined and justified in terms of various factors, but it is mainly to do with the age of learners and the adolescent phase of human development. This phase has always been recognised in society and special provision is usually made in terms of "rites of passage" from childhood to adulthood. This always involves much deeper learning and preparation for adult responsibilities, as distinct from the more care-oriented learning or basic induction into childhood roles/responsibilities.
- In as far as Secondary Education corresponds to learning during the adolescent phase of human development, it is characterised by learning that

caters to the unique requirements of this stage as well as to the diverse requirements for future adult roles and responsibilities. The Secondary curriculum therefore has to cope with the major physical, emotional and psychological changes that the learners are undergoing at this stage. On the other hand this phase also offers important opportunities to build on the growing self-awareness, enthusiasm and dynamism of adolescent learners.

- In some countries there is a status problem associated with vocational subjects that makes it difficult for learners to willingly opt to study these subjects when they have a choice. This goes back to the practice (still prevailing in some systems) of channelling so-called non-academic learners into vocational streams. The main implication of this streaming practice is that these learners are not capable of advancing to university, and should therefore be prepared for a vocation or trade that they will take up on completion of their Secondary Education. Despite such problems the need to better prepare Secondary school leavers for the world of work remains a strong priority for most countries.

- The cost of including vocational subjects in the Secondary curriculum can be prohibitive for some countries. It is therefore difficult to vocationalise the whole Secondary system. Some countries have set up specialised secondary schools that are heavily oriented towards Vocational Education and Training. This approach means that not all learners will have the opportunity to sample or opt for vocational subjects.

- There is a concern in many countries that a Secondary Education that does not deal with the world of work is a handicap. This is because most Secondary students will enter the world of work on completion of their education. There are many innovations designed to bring the world of work into the Secondary classroom, although they do not necessarily involve Vocational Education.

- Some studies have cast doubt on how well Secondary schools can prepare learners for the world of work through the teaching of vocational subjects. The problems involved include badly trained teachers, lack of proper equipment and materials. Because of these difficulties some countries have opted for a "diversification" approach to Secondary education. This introduces vocational subjects into the curriculum in a variety of ways. Typically there is a sampling phase in which all learners have the chance to take one or more vocational subject at an introductory level, so they can understand the field and grow to appreciate the knowledge and skills involved, even if they do not wish to take this up as a vocation. This phase then leads to specialist streams in which those who wish to study these vocational subjects in greater depth have the opportunity to do so, within the limits of what is available in the school.

- The nature of traditional vocational subjects needs to change radically in line with the reality in the world of work, and in order to make these subjects much more attractive to Secondary school learners. The perennial teaching of some subjects like woodwork, metalwork, etc. ensures that the poor image of all vocational subjects will persist for a long time. At the other extreme, the teaching of computers (IT) represents the new and existing face of Vocational Education. Curriculum planners need to work in collaboration with employers and professional to create vocational subjects that are acceptable and can lead to further studies at the tertiary level, if learners choose to pursue that option.

Lessons of the above analysis for the future regarding vocational education include:

- Vocational subjects should be taught in the best way possible for both genders to have a positive impact as pat of the Secondary curriculum. Every school does not have to cater for the teaching of vocational subjects, but could contract out this to the nearest specialist school through appropriate arrangements. Vocational subjects will eventually gain the right status and respect only when they are well taught as existing and worthwhile disciplines.
- Increasingly the distinction between academic and vocational is blurred and irrelevant. The Secondary school curriculum should be alive to this reality, so that learners are offered subjects that are modern and prepare them for life as it is lived out there. Life combines work with continuous learning! That is why we talk of life-long learning. This is what schools should prepare learners for!

Country Reports, Presentations, Discussion and Debate

Country reports presentations, discussion and debate tended to support the points made in the discussion paper, especially on issues to do with competencies, the status of Vocational Educational, and the increased blurring of the distinction between General and Vocation Education.

In Australian (Smith, 2001) "increasingly we are seeing a re-emergence of Aristotle's notion of competence—skill embodying knowledge—hand and mind together". In Russia (Barannikov, 2001) "the concept of key competencies…becomes the pivotal concept around which developments in the content…should be concentrated".

The lack of status of Vocational Education was of great concern to delegates. For example, in Guinea (Kone, 2001) "in the case of repeated failures by a student he/she is dismissed from the General Secondary Education, but he/she is allowed to orient himself/herself towards the technical or professional education". The delegate from Lebanon also pointed the lack of prestige of the Vocational Education when compared to the University stream in her country. This lack of status was common despite many countries having among their objectives for Secondary Education statements similar to that from Mexico (Arancibia, 2001), that is, "To help students join the workforce" or schools such as the Beijing Jingehan School visited by delegates which "has developed a system which connects the academic curriculum with real-life experiences".

Of great interest to participants was the Australian (Smith, 2001) initiative which has "set in place an infrastructure able over time to raise the status of Vocational Education and Training...Vocational Education and Training courses have been repositioned in the state curriculum in a way that eliminates the distinction between general and vocational education...The reforms ensure a rigorous, industry recognised, dual accreditation system...with a capacity for it to [link school, work and/or further training as well as] contribute to university entrance". This Australian development is consistent with Leclercq's (2001) point that "the question of raising the skills level for entry into the labour market is not simply an issue for Technical or Vocational Secondary Education, but also for General Education—not the least because solid, broadly-based knowledge and also generic skills, such as the ability to communicate, now form the basis of all requisite work skills".

Conclusions

After an extensive and wide-ranging discussion and debate on the background and country papers and country presentations, consensus was reached that:

- Instead of accentuating the differences between so-called academic and vocational subjects, the Secondary Education system should focus on links between these subjects and their interdependence in the overall education of adolescent learners of both genders. (Competencies in head and hand).

- Secondary Education is about preparation for life and should reflect the reality of life in the twenty-first century, which encompasses a seamless to-and-fro between continued learning and the world of work (Australia case study).
- The nature of vocational subjects, the way in which they are organised and taught, as well as the recognition given to them, all determine the real status of these subjects in the Secondary school curriculum.
- Secondary Education (including Vocational Education) needs to address not only the human resource needs of the society (China case study), but also the development needs and aspirations of the individual (Russia).
- There is a strong trend in Secondary Education in most countries, to include some element of Vocational Education for all learners. This is sometimes provided as part of a diversified curriculum (Bangladesh) or through themes and inter-disciplinary learning. It can also be provided through guidance programmes, work placement (Australia—NSW) and a cross-curriculum approach (Canada—Quebec).
- Countries are aware of the importance of combining Vocational Education with Secondary Education, and are already experimenting with various ways (e.g. distance learning-Mexico) of providing such joint education to different population groups, including migrants, isolated rural populations and learners in regular Secondary schools. (Mexico).
- Incorporating Vocational Education into Secondary has proved to be very expensive in many countries. As such there has been a trend of poor quality teaching of these subjects, which in turn has resulted in poor status of these subjects. However there has also been a trend of innovative and cost-effective strategies in

some countries, including contracting out the teaching of subjects to nearby specialist schools and centres, or creating different ways of teaching vocational disciplines that are less demanding in terms of equipment, materials and practically trained instructors.

- The trend of life-long learning is becoming clear in many countries, with job requirements constantly changing and people having to move back and forth into education/training and the work place. In some countries, Secondary Education has already started to become adjusted to this reality by developing flexible structures and varied options in their programmes, as well as having stronger links to the world of work.

3. KNOWLEDGE-BASED VERSUS BEHAVIOURAL AND LIFE-SKILLS EDUCATION

Background Document

In her background document Ms. Sonia Bahri argued that acquisition of knowledge is essential for Secondary level students but that it is not sufficient to properly prepare adolescents. Life-skills are also required. She raised the important issues of who takes responsibility for this life-skills education, the possibility of a new role for schools in its provision and the likelihood of utilising other than teachers.

Acquisition of knowledge is essential for Secondary level students.

- Acquisition of knowledge is classically and frequently considered as the main expected outcome of education, and more specifically for formal, General Secondary Education. Knowledge is evolving with scientific and technical progress and needs to be up-dated as well as teaching and learning methods that need to be revised accordingly.

- Everywhere in the world, student evaluation is very often based on knowledge acquisition. This evaluation determines among other things, integration into the Higher Education system. Of course, knowledge covers, in addition to classic disciplines such as mathematics, languages and history, social and contextual issues of common interest.
- Acquisition of knowledge is less a matter of acquiring information than of mastering the instruments of learning, which will enable learners to understand the various aspects of environment and to be able to make sense of reality (including social, economic and scientific realities).

But students in Secondary schools are also adolescents.

- Most of the time, for those involved with education, such as education administrators, school principles, teachers, the population attending Secondary schools are considered only as learners/apprentices, students, pupils or baccalaureate students, but rarely as adolescents. The terminology used by these professionals, that is, to which category we belong, is extremely significant. Students are also rarely considered as participants.
- Adolescence is an age of psychological, emotional and physical changes of great importance. This needs to be recognised and taken into account.

Therefore, acquisition of knowledge is not sufficient to prepare adolescents to cope with life issues and to make choices that could have important impact on their health, and their present and future life as adult citizens.

- According to the Delors Report, "...traditional responses to the demand for education that are essentially quantitative and knowledge based are no longer appropriate. It is not enough to supply each child early in life with a storage of knowledge...; Each individual must be equipped to seize learning opportunities..., both to broaden her or his knowledge, skills and attitudes, and to adapt to a changing, complex and interdependent world".

- The Delors Report articulates education as the four pillars of learning to know, learning to do, learning to be, and learning to live together. The two last pillars are more directly related to the psychological development of the adolescent.
- During the mid-twentieth century, with more massive access to Secondary Education a new phenomenon in the history of humanity appeared: a large number of people working and living together with only one adult (the teacher) for more than eight hours a day. In the past, young people, except in the army, were controlled by bosses or patrons and were not therefore left to themselves. Adult role models were present and available for counselling and guidance at the same time instruction, technical and less frequently general, was provided. An apprentice, for example, who was working in handicraft directly with his boss (master) and had only a few companions with him, was benefiting from an adult behavioural model and occasional advice and guidance, in addition to the technical skills.
- Therefore other specific skills than general, technical or vocational are needed to prepare adolescents to 'learn to be' and learn to 'live together'. Also, research has shown the links that exist between levels of academic achievements and personal and social well being of the adolescent. In brief, there is a need for an adequate education that covers more than training or instruction.

What is this education to be called?

- Several organisations, UN agencies, NGOs, institutions, and national programmes have their own terminology to describe this important issue in education including for example life education, behavioural education, skills for living, family life education, education for citizenship, and life-skills education.

- We will follow the Dakar Framework and use the term 'life-skills'.
- Several national and international initiatives are supporting the development of education in skills for life, or life-skills. These include communication skills, decision-making, preventive and health education, critical thinking, counselling, empathy, and coping with various issues such as stress.

Life-skills education requires appropriate methods for successful implementation.

- Life-skills education does not moralise or use simplistic 'just say no' technique such as in some drug abuse prevention programmes. Instead, highly-skilled educators use interactive and teaching strategies such as role-plays, dramas, discussion and questioning supported by the latest multi-media technology to reinforce learning of relevant skills and information that encourage non-use and safe choices among students. Educators may also use strategies that are in, and/or for, the community.
- The debate is still open about the role of schools in society and to what extent they should be responsible for providing this type of education. Should this education be delivered by schools, and more specifically by Secondary schools, or should it be left to families only and other institutions, or should it be some combination? In some parts of the world, this question does not find an answer. There is still a debate on this subject in many countries such as France. The risk of schools having a strong impact on young peoples' opinions and thoughts is sometimes considered as politically and ideologically dangerous.

- In schools are not coping with these issues, who else will—families, churches/religious institutions, other institutions?

The rapid changes of social, cultural and economic contexts and their impact on the life of adolescents are accentuating these educational requirements.

- For example, drug abuse (including alcohol and tobacco), HIV/AIDS epidemic, violence and suicide among adolescents are rather recent social mass phenomena which pose real dangers for this group of the population. The deep roots of each of these problems are complex and are certainly related to new ways of life, of globalisation, human behaviour and to rapid political and economic and social transformations.
- Gender based discrimination however countries to be a major constraint. The pressure mounts for us to focus on ensuring girls full and equal access to achievement in education of good quality.
- Another social factor is disaggregated families (mono-parental, nuclear families), lack of skills and inexperienced parents who find dealing with adolescents difficult.

There may be a new role for schools but whom in the schools is, or should be, skilled to provide life-skills education?

- schools are optimal places to develop academic but also social/psychological competence and to coordinate efforts of families, teachers, and other school personnel to foster positive attitudes of children and youth, such as:

❑ assist teachers, parents and children to better understand the relationships between child development, academic performance, and social skills in promoting positive attitudes and behaviour;

- ❑ identify, promote and coordinate school and community services and resources that will enhance learning and positive student behaviour and attitudes, including through individual counselling.

- However, many issues such as prevention of HIV/ AIDS and drug abuse are sill taught as disciplines in an academic way. Meanwhile there are issues related to psychological development and behavioural development of children of adolescents that require adequate training of school personnel and appropriate services and facilities or referrals.
- Are teachers skilled to provide life-skills education? What about others such as mentors, tutors and psychologists—especially with the growing shortage of teachers in some countries and the opportunity to work across other sectors such as health and justice in a whole-of-government approach?
- What will be the impact of using others on the school environment, facilities and other school personnel? What will be the costs?

The emerging trends are more and more taken into account in the research arena, in international organisations and in some country's national policies. However, their application remains limited. There in a need maintained Bahri for advocacy for a new vision of educational functions of Secondary Education in the twenty-first century that fully encompasses life-skills education.

Country Reports, Presentations, Discussion and Debate

Country reports, presentations, discussion and debate were quite animated on this issue with strong endorsement for the need to redirect our priorities in Secondary Education more to behavioural, life-skills education. Mexico, Lebanon and Russia provided examples. Mexico (Arancibia, 2001) already has national educational objectives that include: "To allow students to continue their education with a high degree of independence, in and out of school; To provide practical solutions to daily life problems; To promote active and reflexive participation of secondary graduates in social organisations and in political and cultural life of the country". Lebanon (Hamoud, 2001) is moving from a situation "that does not meet the needs of the twenty-first century" of the teacher controlling the class, textbooks as the only resource and teachers and students obsessed by official exams to a New Plan for Educational Reform that seeks citizens who are accepting, respectful, tolerant, work for the development for his society through an education system which includes building personality and developing potentials and abilities. Russia's (Barannikov, 2001) "Strategy of Education Modernisation sees the main results in the graduates readiness and ability to be responsible personally for their own social welfare...and readiness to co-operation and aptitude for creative activity, tolerance of other people's views, communicability, ability to search for and find a constructive compromise".

Useful distinctions were made for the civics area in life-skills education by distinguishing among one's identity as a result of one's heritage, one's ability to tolerate and celebrate differences through multiculturalism and what one values from being a citizen of country through citizenship. Citizenship is in a constant state of being negotiated and thus values involvement.

However concerns were expressed that some schools were not structured for teaching life-long skills or values (Australia) and that some teachers were not capable in this area (Australia) or were not good role models (Guinea). In countries such as Bangladesh (Haque, 2001) "Only 15.8 per cent of the junior secondary school teachers and 36.7 per cent of secondary school teachers have professional qualifications". Also, high student-teacher ratios were seen as militating against effective implications of life- skills programmes (Guinea). Other concerns included increasing advertising pressures (Guinea) and a materialistic youth culture (Russia).

Support was given to the importance of using the students' peers, linkages of the school with others, especially in a 'whole of government' approach, and the new role of teachers as facilitators, provokers, motivators, assessors, and resource centres (Lebanon, Canada).

The Chinese Joint Innovative Project on Raising the Quality of Secondary School Training (Ni Chuanrong, 2001) see also, Yu Fuzeng, 2001) has among its outcomes many that are behavioural and/or involve life-skills, for example: "students have made great progress in moral, intellectual, physical, esthetical, labour and mind…students become highly motivated. They concern themselves with the community…and know how to care for others...they learn about team spirit and cooperation…They are able to study on their own□…"

Conclusions

After an extensive and wide-ranging discussion and debate on the background and country papers and country presentations, consensus was reached that:

- There is recognition that traditional academically based education does not adequately address students' needs in terms of realising their full potential, especially in a context of rapid economic, cultural and social change and gender-based discrimination.
- Schools should take greater responsibility for helping learners acquire values, attitudes and skills (life-skills), given the declining role of other socialising agencies (families, religious bodies).
- The emerging role of teachers (notably as facilitators), their status, integrity and commitment are all essential for implementing life-skills education successfully. The quality of pre-service and in-service teacher training is critical in this regard.
- Teaching methods, school facilities and services should be developed and adapted to provide life-skills education and behavioural oriented education.
- The role of Secondary school principals needs to be consistent with this new reality.

- Education decision makers need to be sensitised and made aware of the consequences of their choices, based, on evidence of such factors as the links between academic success and personal/community well-being.

- A multi-sectoral approach involving government ministries, NGOs local communities, etc., is essential for successful implementation of this kind of education.

4. OTHER

Area of Non-agreement on the Three Themes

Country participants were given numerous opportunities to provide areas where there was not agreement with the above three themes or dilemmas. None were forthcoming.

Other Themes

Country participants were given the opportunity to raise themes not related to the three dilemmas already discussed in depth at the meeting. After persual of country reports and extensive discussion and debate the following additional themes were identified:

- *Inclusive and Compensatory Education:* General Secondary Education should cater for learners who have physical, mental, psychological and social disabilities as well as past academic deficiencies. This means that general Secondary Education should provide for inclusive education and remedial or compensatory education for learners who require such support.

- *Eliminating Gender Disparities:* Gender issues will need to be mainstreamed throughout the education system. Comprehensive efforts are needed to eliminate gender discrimination. Girls in particular will require full and equal access to and achievement in education of good quality. To make this possible, changes in attitudes, values and behaviour are required.

- *Holistic and Participatory Education:* Secondary Education is part of a holistic system of education that embraces all levels from pre-primary to university. This suggests that secondary education should be engaged with other levels in a more constructive manner. It is also important for all cadres to be fully engaged in and accountable for the innovative policies, strategies and practices in Secondary Education. This suggests that Secondary Education should be fully participatory.

- *Strengthening Equity:* Any countries still experience regional disparities and equity gaps (especially between urban and rural areas) in terms of access and quality of education. It is important to explore the main issues of provision, organisation and management of Secondary Education, in order to develop strategies that can reduce these disparities and bridge this rural/urban divide.

- *Information Communication Technology:* Countries need to know about the most effective and efficient use of information communications technology, including for inclusive, compensatory, holistic, participatory, and equitable education. In this regard it may be important to document the Mexican (Arancibia, 2001) and the planned Chinese (Li Lianning, 2001) experience in this area.

5

Identification of Resources and Strategies to Respond to the New Objectives and Functions of Secondary Education and to Manage the Themes or Dilemmas

1. COUNTRY REPORTS, PRESENTATIONS, DISCUSSION AND DEBATE

A number of resource needs and strategies to respond to the new objectives and functions of Secondary Education, and to manage the themes or dilemmas, permeated country reports, presentations, discussion and debate. The following represents just the flavour of this input.

There was very strong endorsement that, as the Guinea delegate stated (Kone, 2001), "the learner and his/her future should be in the centre of concerns". In Lebanon (Hamoud, 2001) the "New Education Reform" sees the learner as active, cooperative and a decision-maker. The new curricula emphasise a student-centred approach. The teacher "is no more the boss…the controller. …he is a provoker, motivator, an assessor, a facilitator, and a centre of resources". Similarly in China (Ni Chuanrong, 2001), "the students" major involvement" is increasingly seen to be at the core of Secondary Education and that "many teachers agree that students should not only be treated as objects of education, but ones to be served as well".

In Australia (Smith, 2001) "the merging of General and Vocational Education has provided significant challenges" to schools, their staff and timetables, welfare structures, and industrial arrangements. These challenges arise because students move to the centre of the education system and they can, for example, attend part-time, be in paid employment and/or in work placements. In Russia (Barannikov, 2001) there is an awareness that, "Severe structuring of basic curricula by a multitude of subjects is undersirable, for it actually blocks integration processes and multiplies subjects unreasonably". In the Chinese Joint Innovative Project on Raising the Quality of Secondary School Training (Ni Chuanrong, 2001) "subject involvement has mobilised students' interests and initiatives and ensured their principal role in learning. As a result, their school work burden has been lightened with remarkable improvement in terms of academic records".

Mexico (Arancibia, 2001) takes the position that a "fairness principle should guide educational offerings in Secondary Education: ...in access, ...thematic content, teaching quality, student permanence, and graduation opportunities". To help achieve this fairness principle, the Mexican Government (Arancibia, 2001) "dares to dream and established a communications network based on satellites to be used to provide basic education for all". As well, a "Telesecondary courses started in 1996. It uses educative television and is for teenagers who, for different reasons, could not join a regular Secondary school. The curriculum at Telesecondary is the same as at the official Secondary school". "Distance Secondary Education... [was also] created for people over fifteen years old who want to start or finish their Secondary school but who are not able to attend regular daily classes".

Quality assurance constituted another area of agreement. As the Bangladesh (Huque, 2001) submission pointed out, "The biggest challenge ... is quality at all levels and in all meanings of the word. Top priority must be given to improving quality ... Acceptance of present quality levels ... would be equivalent to intellectual suicide as a nation and as a people—and would ensure that Bangladesh could not survive and prosper beyond the first few decades of the twenty-first century in an open, interdependent and knowledge and skills-driven global economy".

Strong support was given to the need for (Kone, 2001) "obtaining the engagement and support of the politically responsible" as well as having "competent administrative officials" who used evidence as the basis of their policy making. The Chinese Joint Innovative Project on Raising the Quality of Secondary School Training (Yu Fuzeng, 2001) saw its success depending on three essential conditions: "Support from regional governments", "the importance attached to it by school authorities and teachers"; and, "the combination of administrators, theory researchers and teachers in the forefront of teaching". Li Lianning (2001) also pointed out the requirement to supplement increased government spending on Secondary Education by a variety of approaches including tax incentives, partnerships, donations, sponsorships, and from private investment.

Other Points Raised Included:

- The need to build on existing strengths, for example double shift schools in Lebanon, the Female Secondary Stipend Programme and Community Bank in Bangladesh, distance education in Mexico, and the linkage of General Secondary and Vocational Education and Training in Australia. Wright (2000) concurs with this point when he states, "the first and most important advice for policy makers and professionals who make decisions in education is that they should recognise and appreciate what is positive about their existing education system".
- The need to provide support for school principals and teachers for, as the Bangladesh report (Haque, 2001) points out, a "bottom-up model of innovation is crucial to establishing the demand at classroom level for the necessary supporting inputs (eg. teaching materials, in-service teacher upgrading, etc.) This contrasts with the more typical top-down approach of merely

providing better inputs for the schools on the assumption they will automatically be delivered and used effectively".

- The need for managers to be held accountable for valued, measurable results;
- The structure of the curriculum should not be so tight, either from overcrowding or tight sequencing of subject matter, that it results in students or local needs (such as agricultural education in rural areas) being excluded:
  - ❑ The need to mainstream gender issues throughout the education system;
  - ❑ The effectiveness of whole-of-government approaches that cut across existing Departments such as Education, Health and Justice–an example is the Chinese Community Activity Centres;
  - ❑ The need for identifying an appropriate 'critical mass' in deciding the degree to which the education system can be decentralised, for example the Chinese move back from the town to the country level;
  - ❑ The importance of international organisations such as UNESCO for both providing the ideal we can aspire towards and holding governments accountable for moving towards this ideal.

2. CONCLUSIONS

Participants from Australia, Bangladesh, Canada, Republic of Guinea, Lebanon, Mexico, and the Russian Federation discussed in general terms of resources and strategies needed to respond to the new objectives and functions of Secondary Education and to manage the themes or dilemmas. They agreed that:

- Students are at the centre of any educational reform.

- There are three components to support student's learning—the people, whether educational professionals, parents or community members, the educational policies that offer a framework for what students need to learn, and the infrastructure.
- Member nations should
- For learners
  - ❑ Take into consideration the learners' diversified needs;
  - ❑ Provide learners with knowledge and life-long skills which help enhance their interaction and productivity;
  - ❑ Provide a 'seat' for each learner to guarantee equal opportunity;
  - ❑ Consider learners as the main human resources for a nation's development;
- In respect of resources
  - ❑ Since education contributes to the quality of a nation's human resources, it should be appropriately resourced through adequate budget allocations;
  - ❑ Work hard to provide suitable and adequate school buildings, equipment and material to enhance quality education;
  - ❑ Provide human resources to develop, implement and evaluate curriculum;
  - ❑ Consider the communities' socio-economic needs;
- For teachers and the curriculum
  - ❑ Give priority to pre-service and in-service teacher education;
  - ❑ Ensure that curricula presents its main goals and instructional objective clearly and precisely;

- ❑ Support initiatives to ensure a locally available and professional curriculum development capacity.

Participants from the People's Republic of China discussed in specific terms the resources and strategies needed to respond to the new objectives and functions of Secondary Education and to manage the themes or dilemmas in one country, the People's Republic of China. They agreed on the following priorities and areas where UNESCO may assist:

Priorities

- To ensure policy-makers put enough attention to and stress on the role of Secondary Education, in particular the role played in human resources development and of meeting individual's need of receiving education at a higher level after finishing basic compulsory education.
- To increase the number of senior Secondary schools to satisfy the cohort's need of receiving more education after nine years of compulsory education and guarantee enough resource of enrolment into higher education in the process of China's mass higher education scheme.
- To increase Vocational Senior Secondary schools to satisfy the requirements of the labour market.
- Curriculum reform to enhance its relevance to students' life experience and the local economic and social development.
- To train more qualified Secondary school teachers, especially Vocational teachers.

Areas UNESCO May Assist:

- Organising a government forum discussing Secondary Education;
- Providing successful cases and experience of Secondary Education around the world;

- **Reinforcing the building of information and data base to provide reference materials for considering and comprising the development, administration and implementation of curriculum in Secondary Education;**
- **Consolidating international exchange and cooperation in specific areas such as the integrated curriculum and the learning and teaching style of 'exploratory and discovery learning' emerging in China's practice with the current curriculum reform.**

Finally, A Joint Working Party of the Two Groups Met and Agreed that:

- **Students are at the centre of any education reform;**
- **The following model is broadly representative of the process toward education reform**

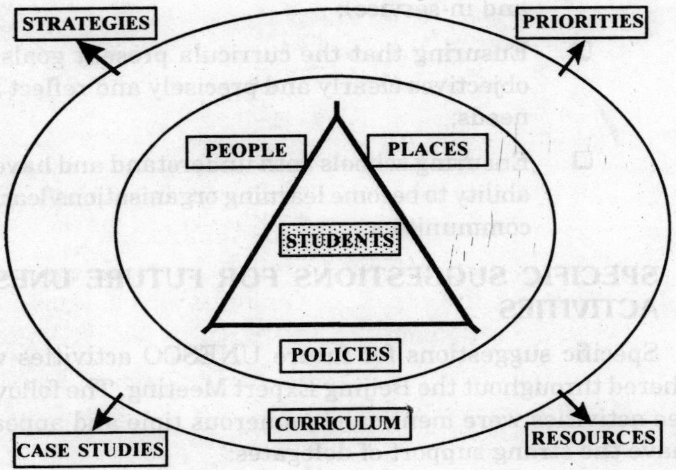

- Member nations seek assistance in attaining the following:
  - ❑ Ensuring that policy-makers stress and give enough attention to Secondary Education;
  - ❑ Reconstructing Secondary Education to ensure a consideration of learners' diversified needs and provide them with knowledge and life-long skills including vocational learning;
  - ❑ Providing access to Secondary Education by providing a place for all learners;
  - ❑ Considering the communities' socio-economic needs (having considered local economic and social development);
  - ❑ Offering appropriate resources for Secondary Education through adequate budget allocations;
  - ❑ Giving priority to teacher training (pre-service and in-service);
  - ❑ Ensuring that the curricula present goals and objectives clearly and precisely and reflect local needs;
  - ❑ Ensuring schools both understand and have the ability to become learning organisations/learning communities.

3. SPECIFIC SUGGESTIONS FOR FUTURE UNESCO ACTIVITIES

Specific suggestions for future UNESCO activities were gathered throughout the Beijing Expert Meeting. The following three activities were mentioned numerous time and appeared to have the strong support of delegates:

- Provide written case studies and/or a data base of best/successful practice in Secondary Education with a focus on issues identified at this meeting
  - ❑ vocational education;

- distance learning and information communications technology;
- life-skills and life-long education;
- discovery learning;
- the changing role of teachers and the use of roles other than teachers in schools;
- pre-service and in-service teacher education and increasing the status of teachers;
- assessment literacy (i.e. having and being able to use assessment with predictive validity) and evidence-informed policy and accountability;
- capacity building or organisational learning/ learning community;
- whole-of-government approaches to policy and practice;
- the balance between administrative, budgeting and curriculum centralisation and decentralisation;
- complementary and alternative provision of resources.

- Organise forums and facilitating international exchange and cooperation in the area of Secondary Education leading to a major World Education Forum on Secondary Education;
- Continue to provide, a vehicle for establishing the ideals for Secondary Education in the twenty-first century and for holding governments accountable for moving towards these ideals.

6

Conclusion

Participants of the Beijing Meeting felt strongly that there is not a clear mandate encouraging UNESCO to focus more directly on Secondary Education. There is also a clear urgency in wanting Secondary Education to be treated as an area in its own right, not simply as an extension of Basic Education or as a filter for Higher Education.

The International Commission on Education for the Twenty-first Century (UNESCO, 1996) stated that, "It is now generally recognised that, for economic growth to take place, a high proportion of the population has to have received secondary education". The Dakar Framework (UNESCO, 2000) agreed stating that, "No country can be expected to develop into a modern and open economy without having a certain proportion of its work force completing secondary education".

In full understanding that education serves more than the economic needs, as well as to facilitate its focus on learning to know, do, be and live together, the Dakar Framework (UNESCO, 2000) also commits countries to "ensuring that the learning needs of all young people and adults are met through equitable access to appropriate learning and life-skills programmes". In order to achieve this and five other goals, the Dakar Framework (UNESCO, 2000) and countries and associations represented at the World Education Forum have pledged twelve actions including to "ensure the engagement and participation of civil society in the formulation, implementation and monitoring of strategies for educational development", to "develop responsive, participatory and accountable systems of educational governance and management", to create safe, healthy, inclusive and equitably resourced educational environments conducive to excellence in learning", to "enhance the status, morale and professionalism of teachers", and to harness new information and communication technologies".

Recently the Ministers of Education of Latin America and Caribbean met and confirmed their commitment to these goals and actions. Secondary Education was seen as a priority and the importance of life-skills was stressed (Cochabamba Declaration, UNESCO, March, 2001): "Secondary education should be a regional priority in those countries that have achieved full access to primary education. The option of encouraging new and flexible forms of learning represents one answer for adolescents and young people living in poverty and exclusion—those who have abandoned formal schooling without having access to quality education". Among their fifty-four recommendations these Ministers (UNESCO, 2001) also asked that, "Special attention be given to affective an emotional factor, due to their great influence on the learning process".

Clearly their is a growing realisation that, as Leclercq (2001) states, "we have to appreciate the need for secondary education to be expanded at a rate faster than some have previously felt necessary". This realisation arises not only as a result of the growing demand for Secondary Education by those completing Basic Education but also because of the dramatic changes in our societies, economic and workplaces.

The Beijing meeting on General Secondary Education in the twenty-first century, which consisted of delegates and experts from ten countries in different regions and varying contexts, from the least developed and most highly populated countries to the developing and developed nations, and balanced in terms of gender, adds yet further weight to the argument by having come to consensus that Secondary Education should be given higher priority.

The Beijing meeting also came to consensus that the objectives and functions of Secondary Education need to be redefined. The meeting identified the contexts and educational trends facing us now and in the future and the implications of these contexts and trends for the objectives and functions of Secondary Education. It identified the main challenges and dilemmas arising from this analysis of the contexts and trends and commenced an identification of the priority areas (including vocational and life-skills education), the resources and the strategies required to respond meaningfully to the new objectives and manage the dilemmas. This work needs to be built upon.

What is important is that in responding to the challenges for Secondary Education in the twenty-first century, the Beijing Meeting saw a need to take a developmental approach and to build on strengths. This desire in consistent with the Dakar Framework's (UNESCO, 2000) position that success is more likely when we build on existing mechanisms.

Wright (2000) points out that "the shift to an era of knowledge and information has given rise to a renaissance in the ideology of education as the main repository of our hopes for the future" and that this "represents a unique opportunity". It is pleasing therefore to find an increasing desire on the part of governments and their educators to want to seek a preferred future for their youth, to differentiate between what is acceptable and what is not. It is the belief of participants at the Beijing Meeting that UNESCO has made a major difference to the provision of Basic Education in the world but it is now time to build on that success by becoming part of, and helping to shape, this desire by governments in Secondary Education.

7

Executive Summary: Meeting Agreements

The UNESCO international expert meeting on General Secondary Education in the twenty-first century held in Beijing, the People's Republic of China, in May 2001 reached consensus that:

- Secondary Education should be given high priority;
- The objectives and functions of secondary education need to be redefined for the twenty-first century.

The meeting then focussed on the major dilemmas Secondary Education is, or will be facing in meeting these redefined objectives and functions. These dilemmas involve the balance between mass and selective schooling, general and specialised (vocational) education and cognitive and behavioural outcomes.

In Respect of Mass and Selective Schooling, Consensus was Reached that:

- Countries should continue to be committed to the goal of mass Secondary Education as a minimum in terms of policy and provision.
- Commitment to universal access to Secondary Education as an aspiration should be maintained with efforts to remove barriers and obstacles as well as build on strengths and opportunities especially for girls.

- Serious attention be given to making adequate provision for those not selected into Secondary Education, those who drop out or leave before completing the cycle and those denied access to their preferred streams.
- Where there is not full transition from Primary to Secondary and/or from lower Secondary to upper Secondary, efforts must be made to accommodate all those who are eligible through alternative provisions. Where this is not possible available places should be allocated equitably and transparently.
- Mass access to Secondary Education will require partnership between governments and other providers (private, NGOs, etc.), but governments should seek to safeguard the interests of learners by ensuring quality standards and maintained by all providers.
- The structure of programmes and steaming practices should be reviewed to offer greater flexibility and choice to learners in the selection process, including the option to return to a preferred stream.
- Future orientation at Secondary should be towards greater quality and diversity of what is provided, more flexibility in the organisation of learning and greater responsiveness to the needs and circumstances of learners.

In Respect of General and Selective (Vocational) Education Consensus was Reached that:

- The Secondary Education system should focus on links between academic and vocational subjects and their interdependence in the overall education of adolescent learners of both genders.
- Secondary Education is about preparation for life and should reflect the reality of life in the twenty-first century that encompasses a seamless to-and-fro between continued learning and the world of work.

- The nature of vocational subjects, the way in which they are organised and taught, as well as the recognition given to them determine their status in the Secondary school curriculum.
- Secondary Education including Vocational Education needs to address not only the human resource needs of the society but also the development needs and aspirations of the individual.
- The is a strong trend in Secondary Education in most countries to include some element of Vocational Education for all learners. Some countries are experimenting with ways of providing such joint education to different population groups, including migrants, isolated rural populations and learners in regular secondary schools.
- Incorporating Vocational Education into Secondary Education can be expensive resulting in poor quality teaching and a lowering of status of these subjects. Innovative and cost-effective strategies to overcome this problem have included contracting out the teaching of subjects to nearby specialist schools and centres or creating different ways of teaching Vocational disciplines that are less demanding in terms of equipment, materials and practically trained instructors.
- As the trend of life-long learning is becoming clear, Secondary Education is adjusting to this reality by developing flexible structures and varied options in their programmes, as well as having stronger links to the world of work.

In Respect of Cognitive and Behavioural Outcomes, Consensus was Reached that:

- There is recognition that traditional academically based education does not adequately address students' needs in terms of realising their full potential, especially in a context of rapid economic, cultural and social change and gender based discrimination;

- Given the declining role of other socialising agencies schools should take greater responsibility for helping learners acquire life-skills;
- The emerging role of teachers (notably as facilitators), their status, integrity and commitment are essential for implementing life-skills education successfully. The quality of pre-service and in-service teacher training is critical in this regard;
- Teaching methods, school facilities and services should be developed and adapted to provide life-skills/behavioural education;
- The role of Secondary school principals needs to be consistent with this new reality;
- Education decision-makers need to be sensitised to the consequences of their choices based on evidence of such factors as the links between academic success and personal and community well being;
- A multi-sectoral approach involving government ministries, NGOs local communities, etc. is essential for successful implementation of this kind of education.

Other Themes Identified by the Meeting that Secondary Education, is or will be, Facing in achieving its New Objectives and Functions included:

- Inclusive and compensatory education;
- Eliminate gender disparities;
- Strengthening equity;
- The effective use of information communication technology.

The Meeting Further Agreed that the Resources and/or Strategies Needed to Respond to the New Objectives and Functions of Secondary Education and to Manage the Themes or Dilemmas include:

- Commencing with the new that students are at the centre of any education reform;

- Understanding that there are three interrelated components to support students' learning—the people, whether educational professional, parents or community members, the educational policies that offer a framework for what students need to learn, and the infrastructure.

Member nations sought UNESCO's assistance in attaining the following in relation to these three interrelated components:

- For students:
  - ❑ Reconstructing Secondary Education to ensure a consideration of learners' diversified needs and provide them with knowledge and life-long skills including vocational learning;
- For teachers, curriculum and school:
  - ❑ Giving priority to teacher education (pre-service and in-service);
  - ❑ Ensuring that the curricula present goals and objectives clearly and precisely and reflect local needs—including socio-economic needs;
  - ❑ Ensuring schools both understand and have the ability to become learning organisations/learning communities.
- For infrastructure and policy:
  - ❑ Ensuring that policy-makers stress and give enough attention to Secondary Education;
  - ❑ Providing access to Secondary Education by providing a place for all learners;
  - ❑ Offering appropriate resources for Secondary Education through adequate budget allocations.

Specific Suggestions for Future UNESCO Activities Centred on:

- Providing written case studies and/or a data base of best/successful practice in Secondary Education with a focus on issues identified at this meeting:

- ❑ Vocational Education,
- ❑ distance learning and information communication technology,
- ❑ life-skills and life-long education,
- ❑ discovery learning,
- ❑ the changing role of teachers and the use of roles other than teachers in schools,
- ❑ pre-service and in-service teacher education and increasing the status of teachers,
- ❑ assessment literacy (i.e. having and being able to use assessment with predictive validity) and evidence-informed policy and accountability,
- ❑ capacity building or organisational learning/ learning community,
- ❑ whole-of-government approaches to policy and practice,
- ❑ the balance between administrative, budgeting and curriculum centralisation and decentralisation,
- ❑ complementary and alternative provision of resources.

- Organise forums and facilitating international exchange and cooperation in the area of Secondary Education leading to a major World Education Forum on Secondary Education;
- Continue to provide a vehicle for establishing the ideals for Secondary Education in the twenty-first century and for holding governments accountable for moving towards these ideals.

References

Arancibia, G.J. (2001). Mexican Secondary Education. Public Education Ministry.

Bahri, S. (2001). Knowledge Based Education Vs Behavioural and Life-skills Education. UNESCO. Paris.

Barannikov, A. (2001). Strategy of School Moderanisation in Russia, General Requirements to Curricula, Federal Law on State Standard of General Education.

Beijing Jingshan School. (2000). Brief Introduction and the 40th Anniversary for Education Reform of Beijing Jingshan School.

Bracey, G. (2001). Research: Test Scores in the Long Run. *Phi Delta Kappan,* 82(8), 637-638.

Brown, P., and Lauder, H. (2001). *Capitalism and Social Progress: The Future of Society in a Global Economy*. Basingstoke: Palgrave.

Education Queensland. (2001). 2010: *A Future Strategy*. Brisbane: Queensland State Education.

Hamoud, S. (2001). Ministry of Education and High Education Lebanon.

Huque, A. (2001). Country Paper: Bangladesh.

Kai-ming Cheng. (2000). Personal Capacity, Social Competence and Learning Together. Canberra: Australian College of

Education. *http://austcolled.com.au/publications/unicorn-1100/4Cheng01.htm*

Kone, M. (2001) Country Paper: Republic of Guinea.

Leclercq, J. (2001). General Secondary Education in the Twenty-first Century: Trends, Challenges and Priorities. UNESCO Working Document.

Levin, H. (1998). High Stakes Testing and Economic Productivity. Paper Presented at the High Stakes K-12 Testing Conference, New York, December 4. *http: www.law.harvard.edu/groups/civilrights/conferences/testing98/drafts/levin.html*

Li Lianning. (2001). Reform of Secondary Education in China.

Mulford, B. (1998). Organisational Learning and Educational Change. In A. Hargreaves, M. Fullan, A. Lieberman, and D. Hopkins. (Eds.). *International Handbook of Educational Change*. Norwell: Kluwer.

Ni Chuanrong. (2001). Subject—Creation—Development: Practice and Theory on JIP Project in Secondary Schools.

OECD. (1998). *Education Policy Analysis*. Paris: OECD.

OECD. (1999). Issues in Secondary Education. Paper for UNESCO Inter-agency Consultation on Secondary Education, Paris, 10/11 June.

Silins, H., and Mulford, B. Leadership and School Results. In K. Leithwood, P. Hallinger, G. Furman-Brown, P. Gronn, B. Mulford, W. Riley, and K. Seashore Louis. (Eds). *Second International Handbook of Educational Leadership and Administration*. Norwell: Kluwer.

Smith, R. (2001). General Secondary Education vs Diversified Vocational Education.

UNESCO. (1996). *Learning: The Treasure Within*. Paris: UNESCO.

UNESCO. (1999a). Inter-agency Consultation on Secondary Education Reform. Paris: UNESCO 10-11 June.

UNESCO. (1999b). Inter-agency Consultation on Secondary Education Reform: Summary Paper. Paris: UNESCO 10-11 June.

UNESCO. (2000). International Working Group on Secondary Education Reform: Report, Paris: UNESCO 7-8 February.

UNESCO. (2000). *World Education Forum: The Dakar Framework for Action*. Paris: UNESCO.

UNESCO. (2001). Cochabamba Declaration, Paris: UNESCO 5-7 March.

Wright, C. (ed.). (2000). *Issues in Education and Technology: Policy Guidelines and Strategies*. London: Commonwealth Secretariat.

Yu Fuzeng. (2001). Implementation and Development of JIP Project in Secondary Schools in China.

Annex—A

List of Participants

Mrs. Gema Jara Arancibia
Directora de Educación Abierta y a Distancia
Dirección General de Materiales y Métodos Educativos
Secretaría de Educación Pública
Mexico City
Mexico
e-mail: *gjara@ilce.edu.mx*

Mr. Anatoly V. Barannikov
Ministry of Education of the Russian Federation
51 ul. Ljusinovskaya
Moscow 113833
Russian Federation
e-mail: *irina@ed.gov.ru*

Mrs. Deborah Gross
Specialist in Educational Sciences
Directorate of Policies and Projects
Services for the English-speaking Community
Ministry of Education
600, Fullum Street
9th Floor
Montréal
Québec
H2K 4L1 Canada
e-mail:
Deborah.Gross@meq.gouv.qc.ca

Mr. Anwarul Huque
Director General
National Academy for Educational Management (NAEM)
Ministry of Education
1, Asian Highway, Palassy-Nilkhet
Dhaka 1205
Bangladesh
e-mail: *naembd@bdcom.com*

Mrs. Samira Hammoud
Head
English Unit
Counselling and Guidance Office
Ministry of Education and Higher Education

UNESCO Palace
Beirut
Lebanon
e-mail:
hammoudsamira@hotmail.com

Mrs. Marie Koné
Professeur,
Chef de Section
Institut National de
Researches et d'Action
Pédagogiques (INRAP)
C/o Commission Nationale
Guinéénne pour
l'UNESCO
Ministére de l'enseignement
supérieur et de
la recherche scientifique
B.P. 964 Conakry
Guinea

Mr. Fuzhi Lin
Principal
Second Middle School of
Beijing Normal University
Nº 12 Xinwai Dajie
Xicheng District
100088 Beijing
People's Republic of China

Mr. Danyuan Liu
Director
Education Research Institute of
Guizhou Province
Nº 129, Heping Road
550001 Guiyang City
People's Republic of China

Mr. Robert Simth
Director, VET in Schools
NSW Department of Education
and Training
35 Bridge Street
Sydney
New South Wales
Australia
e-mail:
bob.smith@det.nsw.edu.au

Mr. Jiayi Wang
Assistant to Chancellor of
Northwest China Normal
University
Northwest China Normal
University
Lanzhou City
730070 Ganshu Province
People's Republic of China
e-mail: *wangjy@nwnu.edu.cn*

International Experts

Mr. Li Lianning
Director General
Department of Basic Education
Ministry of Education
37, Damucang Hutong
Xidan, Beijing 100816
People's Republic of China
e-mail: *liln@moe.edu.cn*

Mr. Cream Wright
Special Adviser/Head of
Education Dept.
Human Resource Development
Division
Commonwealth Secretariat
Marlborough House, Pall Mall
London SW1Y 5HX
United Kingdom
e-mail:
ca.wright@commonwealth.int

National Commission of the People's Republic of China for UNESCO

Mr. Shi Shuyun
Deputy Secretary-General
National Commission of the
People's Republic of China for
UNESCO

37, Damucang Hutong, Xidan
Beijing 100816
Peopole's Republic of China
e-mail:
natcomcn@public3.bat.net.cn

Mr. Du Yue
Director, Programme Division
National Commission of the People's Republic of China for UNESCO
37, Damucang Hutong, Xidan
Beijing 100816
People's Republic of China
e-mail:
natcomcn@public3.bta.net.cn

Mrs. Xiaoping Wang
Deputy Director
Division of Programme and Planning
National Commission of the People's Republic of China for UNESCO
37, Damucang Hutong, Xidan
Beijing 100816
People's Republic of China
e-mail: *wangxp@moe.edu.cn*

UNESCO

Mr. Qian Tang
Director
Division of Secondary, Technical and Vocational Education
UNESCO
7, place de Fontenoy
75352 Paris 07 SP
France
e-mail: *q.tang@unesco.org*

Mrs. Sonia Bahri
Chief
Section for General Secondary Education
Division for Secondary, Technical and Vocational Education
UNESCO
7, place de Fontenoy
75352 Paris 07 SP
France
e-mail: *s.bahri@unesco.org*

Ms. Maki Hayashikawa
Officer-in-Charge/Education Officer
UNESCO
5-15-3 Jianguomenwai
Waijaogongyu
Beijing 100600
People's Republic of China
e-mail:
m.hayashikawa@unesco.org
OR *beijing@unesco.org*

Ms SUN Lei
National Programme Officer for Education
UNESCO
5-15-3 Jianguomenwai
Waijaogongyu
Beijing 100600
People's Republic of China
e-mail: *l.sun@unesco.org*

Mr. Bill Mulford
UNESCO Consultant
3, Park Heights
Feinnes Crescent
The Park
Nottingham
United Kingdom NG7 1ER
e-mail:
billmulford@hotmail.com

Annex—B

GENERAL SECONDARY SCHOOL EDUCATION IN THE TWENTY FIRST CENTURY: TRENDS, CHALLENGES AND PRIORITIES

Working Document

Prof. Jean-Michel Leclercq, Ph.D.
UNESCO, Paris

1. KEY PROBLEMS

It is proposed that three key problems, which are not only fundamental but interdependent, be subjected to analysis: the impact of the new social and economic context, the ways in which attendance has been increased and the consequence of that increase, and the forms of modernisation to be considered. There is justification on at least two counts for taking these as the key problems. First, all three correspond to deep-seated developments, which, if not already underway, are at least foreseeable—developments connected with essential issues of general secondary-school education, either in its aims or its modes of operation, elements which are almost always at issue when concern to adopt new directions and scenarios arises. Second, at the methodological level, the analysis of each of these problems simultaneously entails the assessment of current situations, the making of future projections or comparisons between the situations in the various education systems, and the foregrounding, in each case, of a particular perspective, given the nature of the object and its specific characteristics. In examining the impact of context, we may clearly expect to see assessments and comparisons accorded a leading role, whereas in examining efforts and modernisation we shall rightly expect to see a forward-looking perspective, doubtless as a result of the disappointing assessments to which many attempts at innovation give rise.

The Impact of the New Economic and Social Context

We might consider the need to accord particular attention to the impact of developments in the economic and social context—developments which are, as we know, always crucial to any kind of education or training.

It is, however, beyond doubt that these developments have come to have an even more decisive impact on general secondary-school education, on account of the role this is expected to play both in training the personnel required for the economy and in training the citizens who have to form today's societies. The question of raising the skills level for entry into the labour market is not simply an issue for technical or vocational secondary education, but also for general education—not least because solid, broadly-based knowledge and also generic skills, such as the ability to communicate, now form the basis of all requisite work skills. It also falls to general secondary education to develop in young people those attitudes which contribute to the proper functioning of societies, such as civic sense or tolerance. These points were highlighted by the International Commission on Education for the Twentieth-first Century, which stated: "It is now generally recognised that, for economic growth to take place, a high proportion of the population has to have received secondary education"[1]. It was also argued, at the Dakar World Education Forum, that: "No country can be expected to develop into a modern and open economy without having a certain proportion of its work force completing secondary education"[2]. The same Forum's report on

---

1 Learning: The Treasure Within *(Paris: UNESCO, 1996)*

2 *The Dakar Framework for Action* (Paris: UNESCO, 2000) paragraph 34.

Europe and North America pointed out that: "with the development of knowledge and of its influence on the lives of people, basic education takes more time: in our countries, it covers at least lower secondary education"[3]. It is, however, probable that this standpoint will soon cease to be the preserve of the most prosperous countries and that more and more regions will come to share, it, given the deep and rapid changes the economic and social context is set to undergo.

As a result, there is need both of a forward-looking approach to the economic and social context and of a vision for general secondary education in the future. In particular, we have to appreciate the need for secondary education to be expanded at a rate faster than some have previously felt necessary. For example, a development of production techniques in which intellectual operations take precedence over manual operations on account of the massive introduction of new technologies may lead to questioning the wisdom or retaining vocational training within the lower secondary school, when this may deprive pupils of the requisite range of general knowledge. In time, vocational training in the upper secondary school may ultimately come to be questioned in a similar way, as happened in Japan in the 1980s.

It goes without saying, however, that the analysis of context cannot merely consist in identifying overwhelming trends to which we must necessarily submit. Among those trends, we have to differentiate between what is acceptable and what is not. Only if general secondary education stands impotently by, or colludes with the development, will unscrupulous productivism or unbridled consumerism result. And it must indeed show its determination to help young people to resist all the forms of excess or deviance in the surrounding environment.

We should not forget, too, that secondary education provides its own context. It is always possible, through system effects or by the action of pressure groups, for the administrative and pedagogical organisation of that education to set itself up

3 *"Regional Framework for Action. Europe and North America", February, 2000.*

as the equivalent of an external, independent reality, promoting certain conceptions or practices and thwarting others. This explains, for example, why thoroughly sound project may fail for want of sufficient understanding of the attitudes and behaviour of education officers, teachers, families or pupils. It may be that this phenomenon applies more to general secondary education than to other sectors, on account of the importance society attributes to that sector or the importance it attributes to itself under the influence of a persistent elitism.

The relations between general secondary-school education and its context are, then, highly complex. There must be a concern to investigate and decipher these relations, both in order to be able to explain situations as products of natural, legitimate influences, and also to detect excesses or anomalies which may generate what are in some cases tragic misconceptions and illusions.

Mass Secondary Enrolment, Democratisation and Equity

In the operation of general secondary education over the last two or three decades the most striking phenomenon has been the very great increase in enrolment levels.

As can be seen from the statistics in the table below, in the Member States represented at this meeting the increase between 1970 and 1997 has been spectacular. In many countries, total enrolments have risen by a factor of two or three, and in some cases far more. It is evident that this process is universal among the countries concerned, since it occurs in both the richest and the most deprived of them. And it shows up even more clearly when we remember that, in the countries of Europe as a whole, enrolment figures in upper secondary education have virtually doubled since 1980.

This development has comparable causes in the sample of systems selected for examination at this meetings and on a much wider scale. One essential factor in the shift to mass secondary education has been the inclusion of lower secondary-school education in compulsory schooling. In almost all cases those countries concerned to make up for previous backwardness in this area, such as Bangladesh and China, have extended the length of compulsory education to nine years. However, a similar extension of compulsory schooling has also occurred in recent years in many industrialised countries, showing the same concern on the part of governments to provide young people with the basic education required by the changes in the economy and society. For identical reasons, in those years of upper secondary education which are not part of compulsory schooling, families—often encouraged by governments—choose to have their children carry on their studies. Though this trend is much marked in the northern hemisphere, it also exists in the South.

In these conditions, it is quite clear that the profile and purposes of general secondary-school education change profoundly. It is no longer reserved, as in the past, for the minority of the most fortunate youth. Nor is it any longer the prime aim of secondary education to afford access to higher studies, even if that remains very much a goal. It must provide the skills with which to enter working life, and must in many cases do so for the majority of pupils. Many still begin their working lives at the end of lower secondary education, but increasingly often they now do so at the end of upper secondary schooling. With the advent of mass secondary enrolment, we have seen a different form of secondary education established, with a view clientele and new missions to fulfil.

However, it is equally obvious that this—theoretically compulsory—enrolment in lower secondary, or voluntary enrolment in upper secondary, education is far from representing a merely utilitarian decision on the part of governments or users, dictated by the demands of the country (and by a concern to escape unemployment, in particular). They are also looking for a more democratic, more equitable operation of the education system, in which access to secondary education no longer restricted to an elite or to the most privileged social groups. This is particularly the case with lower secondary education, which has become an integral part of a common core of education—something long called for in many countries across the whole political spectrum and within all social groups. But the attitude towards upper secondary education is not radically different. Access to "high school" is regarded as a symbol of social advancement virtually the world over. This explains the disaffection which may be felt with vocational training at the upper secondary level—that form of training not being seen as part of "proper high-school education". How else are we to explain the low enrolment figures in vocational education in the table below or the fact that enrolment figures for such training did not rise in Europe until the continent experienced a long period of very high unemployment among the 18-24 age-group?

We must, however, remind the reader that the actual situations produced by the expansion of general secondary-school may be very far removed from the advances in democratisation and equity expected.

Certain groups are still frequently sidelined. As is well known, outside Europe, North America and Japan, access to general secondary-school education and, even more to technical education remains difficult for girls. And everywhere, irrespective of sex, children from economically deprived or socially stigmatised groups and those suffering physical or mental handicaps suffer overt or concealed forms of segregation. Conversely, the systematic provision of general secondary-school to all youngsters may leave some facing patterns of study which expose them to failure, or bring them very limited opportunities for socio-professional inclusion. When this is the case, instead of providing a fairer distribution of opportunity, the expansion of general secondary-school education may produce now social divisions.

Furthermore, mass secondary enrolment has not always been accompanied by allocation of the necessary resources to provide adequate conditions for learning. There may not be a sufficiently close-knit network of educational establishments to prevent children from having to make long, inconvenient journeys to school. Some subjects may be neglected or ignored for want of sufficient staff, or staff with the necessary skills, to teach them. A shortage of buildings or teachers may mean classes are overcrowded. These are defects which would be harmful in any conditions, but they are particularly harmful for those we might term the "new pupils" of the secondary sector, who need the best possible school environment to adapt to a new world and achieve good results in it. Here, again, these

problems mainly affect lower secondary education, and we know that the considerable difficulties sometimes experienced there relate largely to a lack of material and human resources being brought on stream to deal with the many problems generated by the introduction of compulsory enrolment. Upper secondary education is, however, already facing the same problems, and will do so increasingly as rolls increase.

Enrolment in Secondary Education 1970-1997

Country	1970	1980	1990-1991	1993-1997
Bangladesh		T. 3,156,119	T. 2,142,335	
		F. 606,913	F. 1,070,000	
Canada	T. 1,636,913		T. 2,292,497	T. 2,505,389
	F. 799,141		F. 1,118,112	F. 1,218,403
China	T. 26,482,976		T. 52,385,600	T. 71,883,000
			F. 21,706,500	F. 32,530,00
			V. 2,150,400	
Guinea	T. 59,918		T. 85,942	T. 153,661
	F. 13,064		F. 20,929	F. 39,449
	V. 2,013		V. 8,202	
Lebanon	T. 159,871		T. 248,097	T. 347,850
	F. 64,141		F. 131,352	F. 179,629
	V. 2,590		V. 37,403	
Mexico	T. 1,584,342		T. 6,704,297	T. 7,631,605
	F. 609,969		F. 3,163,293	F. 3,407,756
	V. 423,584			
Russia	T. 11,351,000		T. 12,363,000	T. 12,424,000
	F. 5,735,000		F. 6,300,000	F. 6,399,000
	V. 1,399,000		V. 1,252,000	V. 1,007,000
South Africa	T. 542,194		T. 2,742,105	T. 3,749,449
	F. 264,461		F. 1,474,611	F. 2,039,551

Key: T— total enrolment

F— female enrolment

V— enrolment in vocational secondary education

Source: *UNESCO Statistical Yearbook* (except in the case of Bangladesh, where the sources used are national statistics).

The Need for Moderanisation and Innovation

A third aspect of general secondary education with which we must concern ourselves is the modernisation of that education through major innovations in its modes of operation and teaching methods. These are processes from which it cannot really remain aloof, given the many adaptations currently being required of it—adaptations it would hardly be possible to make without breaking with approaches which have often remained unchanged for many years. Modernisation has to be brought about if the many adaptations required are to be achieved: adaptation to the development of knowledge and to technological advance; adaptation to secondary education's new clientele; adaptation to the new roles that education has to play in societies. Modernisation and innovation must be achieved in practically every sector.

First and foremost, the syllabus needs to be modernised. The place of certain disciplines in the syllabus must be upgraded—disciplines which have always been taught, but which today require particular attention, either to update their content, as in the sciences and technology, or to raise their profile, as in the case of language-teaching. Room has also to be made for subjects which have until now been virtually ignored, such as the new information and communication technologies, civics, and inter-cultural or sexual education, not to mention increased provision for artistic culture or physical and sporting activities. But we have even to rethink the notion of syllabus or curriculum so that young people may benefit from teaching and education in which all the elements are inter-linked and related to all the components of their person and their existence. This is all the more necessary when preparation for working life has become as important in secondary education as preparation for higher studies. And this problem by no means relates merely to the countries of the South—where a secondary qualification is supposed to open other doors than those of the university. In the North, at least 20 per cent of pupils do not obtain a leaving qualification and have to face career paths which may often be complex and arduous. Secondary education must equip them too with other assets than a passport to university.

We are also increasingly aware that changes in content must be accompanied by changes in teaching methods. The methods which prevailed in the past were based largely on teacher authoritarianism and pupil passivity. The disadvantages of these methods are now clear for all to see. First, they are detrimental to a section of the school population which is poorly prepared to fit into a mould which favours theoretical and intellectualist styles entirely alien to the approaches prevalent in the social groups from which a large fraction of secondary pupils now come. But, most importantly, these methods are ill-adapted to the conditions for knowledge- and skills-acquisition as revealed by the cognitive sciences; they are also inappropriate in view of the possibilities opened up by the new vehicles of information and communication. There can be no passive reception. It is by active discovery and exchange that we learn. We can no longer be content with teaching through unidirectional messages, teaching focussed solely on the pupil's brain. We have now to concern ourselves with the whole person and his/her diversity.

We could not hope to do this either if secondary schools did not also radically modify their modes of operation. This involves, first, the adoption of new ways of working by teachers to impart the requisite dynamism and flexibility to learning-failing which, teachers and pupils alike run the risk of delusion, boredom and failure. Second, it involves the formation of educational teams which are open to the entire educational community, and hence not merely made up of teachers. This is one of the essential conditions for responding to pupil needs in all areas, giving them all the time they need and showing an ability to listen. It also involves a new governance of schools, in which democratically based rules of conduct—and, above all, rules of life-should prevail—rules adopted as far as possible through dialogue and participation. It is difficult to see how we can otherwise offer the requisite secondary education to people who are not the pupils of yesteryear, but young men and women determined to assert their independence and maturity.

It doubtless remains for us to ask whether lower and upper secondary education do not call for different approaches. Are there not still, particularly in lower secondary education, adolescents who ought to be shown a better lead (though this does not mean abandoning recourse, where necessary, to stricter forms of discipline)? A similar question arises with regard to what is taught. In so far as, in most education systems, lower secondary education now forms part of basic education, it seems natural that it should involve the assimilation of a single syllabus by all pupils. By contrast, as the Report of the International Commission on Education for the Twentieth-first Century stresses, upper secondary-school education must be highly diversified. It should "be the time when the most varied talents are revealed and flourish"[4]. Yet it is increasingly questionable whether lower secondary education can continue to hold to an authoritarian model for its operation and a unitary model for its curriculum-features which are always likely to pose problems for some pupils. The recent measures of France to introduce more flexibility into its "common school" model are sympathetic in this regard.

Most aspects of modernisation and innovation give rise to comparable degrees of hesitancy. Indeed, this is a field in which there are many more questions than answers. Modernisation programmes have in many cases had to be redrafted in mid-stream, as all the Member States represented at this meeting will be aware. The outcomes of these programmes are often disappointing on account of the lengthy time-spans or unwieldy compromises involved. Teacher training has also seen many reform projects, but it is difficult to avoid an impression that little actual progress is being made. When an initiative leads to the conclusion that teacher training must "include, among other things...an input from other disciplines (than the one taught)...sensitisation to linguistic and cultural diversity...learning teamwork...discovering interactivity...and acquiring an awareness that pupils today are no longer willing to receive an education in the traditional sense,"[5] and when

---

4 *Learning: The Treasure Within (Paris: UNESCO, 1996).*

5 *La Formation des Enseignants* (Paris: La Documentation Française, 2000).

one finds a whole string of similar viewpoints expressed,[6] one is both convinced of the strength of identical concerns and yet uneasy about the actual effect achieved.

We are not, then, seeing at all clearly the emergence of those "learning organisations" which secondary schools ought, in the view of the OECD, to become if they are to meet the challenges of the new millennium, particularly as regards entry into lifelong learning. However, even more modest ambitions seem far from being satisfied. Educational teams exist more on paper than in reality. And few of their members are non-teaching staff or come from outside the school. More generally, secondary schools are not places where human resources are satisfactorily managed, even though the educational world might be taught a much more favourable setting than business for providing careers in which everyone, through the full and free deployment of their skills, would be recognised at their true worth and feel fulfilled by their work.

A further illustration of reticence and overcautiousness can be seen in the fate reserved for the self-government of schools. The idea that this is a timely development—and one which needs to be reinforced—is a practically unchallenged. But self-government generally remains limited because it seldom extends to financial autonomy and, so far as the syllabus is concerned, when it comes to deciding timetables and the subject to be taught, restrictive regulations usually apply. Conversely, self-government has only to increase for concern to surface immediately about the prospects of preserving sufficient coherence in the education system or avoiding disparities which generate inequalities in educational provision in the secondary sector.

Clearly, a vision for a secondary education modernised by thoroughgoing innovation still remains to be forged—innovation not merely confined to incorporating new resources, such as

---

6 *As in the Canadian Report,* Enhancing the Role of Teachers in a Changing World *(Council of Ministers of Education, Canada, 1996), p. 37.*

information technology, but actively employing those resources to change to practices and behaviour of teachers and pupils.

2. REFORMS AND REFORM STRATEGIES

The foregoing thoughts lead on naturally to the view that a serious redesign of secondary education is necessary and that such projects are in danger of running into sufficient obstacles, such as the complexity of the problems to be tackled or the resistance posed by existing situations.

The difficult nature of educational reforms has, in fact, become a recurring theme among educational decision-makers and practitioners. One recent writer revealingly entitled a book on the subject: *Education: An Impossible Reform*?[7] Another, in a study on the question of educational reform in sub-Saharan Africa between 1960 and 2000, stressed the ineffectiveness of efforts at change made over almost half a century[8].

It is probable too, however, that the weariness felt at failed reform projects has provided a stimulus to reflection on the conditions in which reforms may best succeed and, more precisely, on the processes and strategies to be adopted to that end[9].

This reflection has highlighted the following points:

A reform always requires a detailed preparatory research phase, which may extend over several years. This may seem a major obstacle in situations where reform is urgently needed, but it would be better to resort, where necessary, to a number of temporary individual measures, amounting virtually to mere treatment of the symptoms, than hastily to launch a poorly prepared project of general reform which is likely to have very harmful consequences of a deep and lasting nature.

---

7 *Pierre Laderrière,* L'enseignement, une réforme impossible? Analysis comparée *(Paris: L'Harmattan, 1999).*

8 Amara Fofana, *La Problématique de la réforme de l'éducation en Afrique Subsaharienne 1960-2000,* Unpublished Study, BREDA/Dakar.

9 In this Connection, see *Strategies for Educational Reform: from Concept to Realisation* (Strasbourg, Council of Europe, 2000).

This research phase must also be a phase of consultation with all the parties involved in the reform. The age of top-town reform in past. Today, there must be dialogue between the decision-makers and their partners (local communities, teachers, families and, increasingly now, the pupils-at least in the upper secondary sector). This approach of arriving at a consensus through consultation may take a considerable time, not least because of the important of information and communication required.

If time is needed for the preparation of reforms, it is also needed for their application, since gradual introduction of reforms is far preferable to immediate, across-the board implementation, which may produce over-ambitious expectations or violent changes in practice of a kind likely to spark all manner of resistance.

This is also why, in the long process of implementing reform, one should not be afraid to review it or, indeed, to reform itself if some of its elements seem to require revision because they are either ineffective or harmful. This, however, assumes a process of running evaluation of the reform, which is not always present.

The precautions which must accompany the preparation and implementation of reforms lead us also to ask what their pattern and scope should be? Should we consider reforming the whole of an education system at all levels and in all sectors? Or should we not have much more limited aims, relating to a well-defined area? Opinions on this question continue to differ, but some trends can be identified. Awareness of the complexity and difficult of any reform suggests at least that reforms should be made in a particular sector and should be phased in gradually. This is preferable to launching a thoroughgoing reform at a stroke. Attention should also be given to the inevitable inter-dependency of elements. There is little sense changing teaching structures or syllabuses without a parallel reform of teacher training. But it is also becoming clearer that reforms relating to contents and methods seem to have much greater impact than reforms of the administrative or teaching structures. This explains why we are much more likely to find reforms of the syllabus or of teacher training in the secondary sector today than structural reorganisations of lower or upper secondary education. All in all, it seems to be accepted that the way of preparing and carrying out reform is an important as its content, and that a reform is, first and foremost, a strategy for change.

At all events, to be effective a reform has to meet two imperatives. It must set clearly defined, clearly prioritised objectives, which are not a shopping-list of measures but a systematic set of priorities, as few in number as possible. It must lay down the strategies to be implemented to achieve these objectives, with all that this involves in terms of the scheduling of successive interventions and permanent assessment to evaluate the results attained and those which remain to be achieved. There can be no doubt either their these demands are even more pressing in secondary education, where situations and issues have to be addressed in all their complexity, given the large numbers of people now involved and the interconnectedness of the many problems faced.

Source and Courtesy: UNESCO, Paris

Annex—C

KNOWLEDGE-BASED EDUCATION VERSUS BEHAVIOURAL AND LIFE-SKILLS EDUCATION

Ms. Sonia Bahri, Ph.D.
Chief of the Section for General Secondary Education,
UNESCO, Paris

Introduction

Secondary schools were created as formal educational institutions in the 19th century, in countries starting industrialisation, with a view to providing an elite of young people with the relevant knowledge in several disciplines considered as necessary to both contribute to the progress of science and techniques and in colonial countries, to the expansion and control of territories.

At that time, secondary schools, like other schools, were conceived to meet the needs of society; their primary aim was to 'produce' people with the academic knowledge required to access University and to contribute to the economic, administrative and political life of the country.

Since that period, a despite changes in societies, acquisition of knowledge through a certain number of disciplines is classically and frequently still considered as the main expected out-come of education, and more specifically of formal, general secondary education.

The acquisition of knowledge is essential for secondary level students but that acquisition of knowledge is not sufficient to prepare adolescents to cope with life issues. Life skills education is needed as part of the new for secondary schools in the 21st century.

1. Acquisition of Knowledge is Essential for Secondary Level Students

Of course, knowledge covers, in addition to classic disciplines such as mathematics, languages, history, and geography, social and context issues of common interest. But this knowledge is evolving with scientific and technical progress. Knowledge is becoming more and more complex and needs to be continually up-dated. Teaching and learning methods also need to be revised accordingly. It should be noted, though, that acquisition of knowledge is less a matter of acquiring information than of mastering the instruments of learning. These instruments enable learners to understand the various aspects of the environment and to be able to make sense of reality, including social, economic and scientific realities.

There is no doubt that secondary schools, with trained teachers in each discipline, are the most appropriate places for learners to acquire this essential knowledge. However, secondary education addresses learners between 12-19 years old, which corresponds to the crucial period of adolescence. Adolescence is an age of psychological, emotional, and physical changes of great importance.

It is important to note that most of the time, for those involved with education, such as curriculum planners, administrators, school principals, and teachers, the population attending secondary schools are considered only as learners/ apprentices, students, pupils or baccalaureate students, but rarely as adolescents. They are also rarely considered as participants.

In addition to the critical age of adolescence, large numbers of youth in every region of the world are increasingly finding themselves unequipped to deal successfully with challenges, such as those presented by unemployment, the HIV/AIDS pandemic, the scourge of drugs and exclusion, and all in a context of rapid economic, social, cultural and technological change resulting from globalisation.

2. Acquisition of Knowledge is not Sufficient to Prepare Adolescents to Cope with Life Issues

The situation facing young people in today's world clearly shows that acquisition of knowledge through academic education is not sufficient to prepare adolescents to cope with life issues and to make choices which could have important impact on their health, and their present and future life as adult citizens.

As it is emphasised in the Delors Report (1996), "...traditional responses to the demand for education that are essentially quantitative and knowledge based are no longer appropriate. It is not enough to supply each child early in life with a storage of knowledge (...); Each individual must be equipped to seize learning opportunities (...), both to broaden her or his knowledge, skills and attitudes, and to adapt to a changing, complex and interdependent world".

This report articulates education as 4 pillars:

- *Learning to know*, by combining a sufficiently broad general knowledge with the opportunity to work in depth on a small number of subjects. This also means learning to learn.

- *Learning to do*, in order to acquire not only an occupational skill but also, more broadly, the competence to deal with many situations and work in teams. It also means learning to do in the context of young people various social and work experiences which may be informal, as a result of the local or national context, or formal, involving courses, alternating study and work experiences.

- *Learning to Live Together,* by developing an understanding of other people and an appreciation of interdependence, carrying out joint projects and learning to manage conflicts, in a respect of the values of pluralism, mutual understanding and peace.

- *Learning to be*, so as better develop one's responsibility and be able to act with ever greater autonomy, judgement and personal responsibility.

These two last pillars, "learning to live together" and "learning to be" are less related to acquisition of knowledge, know-how and cognitive skills and more directly related to the psycho-social development of adolescents and to values, attitudes and behaviours.

However, research (for example Mulford and Silins, 2001) has shown the links which exist between levels of academic achievements and personal and social well being of the adolescents. In other words, if secondary school students have adequately developed their personality, their judgement and personal responsibility, if they are more comfortable with their bodies and their health and in their relations with others, they will have more chances to have better academic learning achievements.

On the basis of the assumption that adolescents should "learn to be" and to "live together", there is a need for the provision of a more relevant education which moves beyond the acquisition of knowledge and technical/vocational skills, and moves beyond training or instruction.

The questions which arise (or should be raised) are:

- What should this education be called?
- How can education and more specifically secondary education effectively ensure provision of these other types of learning in a holistic and harmonious manner with the two other types?
- What will be the implications for schools in terms of teaching/learning methods, training of teachers and other schools personnel, school management, and so on?

3. The Need for Life Skills Education

Several organisations, UN agencies, NGOs and national programmes have acknowledged the importance of this broader kind of education. They variously term this education:

- Life education
- Behavioural education
- Skills for living
- Skills for life education
- Education for citizenship
- Life skills education

We will use the term *life-skills* as it is the term used in the Dakar (UNESCO, 2000) framework for action. During the World Education Forum, the international community committed itself to achieving six main goals and among them, "ensuring that the learning needs of all young people (...) are met through equitable access to appropriate learning and *life skills-programmes*." (goal 3) and "improving all aspects..."

The Dakar framework for action clearly acknowledges that life skills education is all part of quality education and that it should both be provided to young people at secondary level and be therefore measurable as a learning outcome.

To reiterate, several national and international initiatives around the world are supporting the development of education for life skills. These include an important number of skills necessary for life. It includes skills such as communication skills, decision-making, critical thinking, environmental education, preventive and health education, counselling, empathy, and coping with various issues such as stress. One could classify these skills in categories but the list should not be exhaustive as skills required will depend on the context or situation where this education takes place and which varies from one country to another, form one social and cultural context to another.

This kind of education requires specific teaching/learning methods for successful implementation. For instance, this education does not moralise or use simplistic 'just say no' techniques, as was the case for a contested method used for drug abuse prevention. Instead, highly-skilled educators use interactive and teaching strategies such as role-plays, dramas, discussion and questioning which could be supported by the latest multi-media technology to reinforce learning of relevant skills and information that encourage responsible and safe choices among students. Educators may also use strategies that involve in and for the community. It should, of course, be integrated in an appropriate manner in the curriculum.

4. A New Role for Secondary Schools in the 21st Century?

While some countries have developed life-skills programmes in the curriculum of their formal secondary education system, the debate is still open about the role of schools in society and to what extent they should be responsible for providing this type of education.

This debate on the role of schools in the education of the individual is not a new one. It started in the 18th Century and was at the heart of the 'philosophic des lumières' opposing Voltaire and Condorcet views to those of Rousseau and Kant.

Should this kind of education be believed by schools and more specifically by secondary schools or should it only be left to families and other institutions, or should it be some combination?

In some parts of the world, this question does not find an answer. The debate continues. The risk of shaping schools having a strong impact on young people's opinions and thoughts is sometimes considered as politically and ideologically dangerous.

However, it seems clear that the question which needs to be raised today, beyond any philosophical consideration should be the following: if schools are not coping with these issues, who else will?

The role of families in the educational process, and more specifically in life-skills education, has progressively declined.

The size of families has been drastically reduced to become a nuclear or even in many cases a mono parental family with a father frequently absent.

In addition to this recent social phenomenon, parents feel inexperienced or unskilled and find it difficult discussing, with their adolescents children about sensitive issues such as violence, suicide, drug abuse, and HIV/AIDS prevention.

Today, it is recognised that the media and more specifically television, which is very often watched by children and young people several hours a day has an influence on adolescent's values, attitudes and behaviours.

Despite the impact of the medias on adolescents, schools remain potentially an important source of influence. Since the mid-fifties the number of children attending secondary education in the world has multiplied by ten-40 million students in 1950 compared to more than 400 million today (World Education Report, 2000). It is expected that the rate of enrolment of adolescents at secondary level is going to increase significantly as a result of the implementation of the Education for All initiative to promote basic education.

The place schools occupy in the daily environment of adolescents argues in favour of the role they should play in helping people acquire positive attitudes and behaviour and make responsible choices for their future through an appropriate life-skills education.

Schools are therefore optimal places to develop academic but also life skills education. They are also an optimal place to liaise with other sectors (for example, health, justice, police) and coordinate efforts of families, teachers, and other school personnel to foster positive attitudes of children and youth. Examples could include:

- Assist teachers, parents and children to better understand the relationships between adolescent development, academic performance, and social skills in promoting positive attitudes and behaviour;

- Identify, promote and coordinate school and community services and resources that will enhance learning and positive student behaviour and attitudes.
- Associate professionals from other sectors, such as doctors and nurses, police officers, judges, to preventive education programmes.

Teachers are not always adequately trained for this kind of education. Some argue that they are used to teaching like they have been taught. Many issues, such as education for citizenship, education to prevent violence, tobacco use prevention, are still taught in an academic way although they are obviously issues related to psychological and behavioural development of children and adolescents in specific contexts. Teachers need appropriate and up-dated training both at pre-service level and on-the-job. The changing role of teachers at secondary level, including for life skills education, is now more seriously taken into consideration by several countries in their policies for teacher training and by the Teacher Unions.

Teachers recognise the importance of not being left alone in providing life-skills education to their students and the need to work in team with other school personnel. An adequate training for them is also called for as well as appropriate services and facilities or referrals are required.

Among the other school personnel, the role of school counsellors, with a specific psychological training, will notably through individual counselling, by extremely significant to develop secondary schools students' life-skills. Other actors, sometimes called 'new actors', such as mentors and tutors, working with a limited number of students, could also play an important role, especially with a growing shortage of teachers in some countries.

Many other issues, linked with the role of secondary schools in the provision of life skills programmes, have to be raised and discussed within an interdisciplinary approach and perspective. These issues include:

- What will be the impact on school environment and facilities?

- What will be the new required functions of school leaders?
- What will be the costs?
- What will be the long term savings in term of social costs?

Conclusion

These emerging and inter-related trends and challenges are taken into account increasingly by UNESCO and other international organisations, in and in some countries' national policies, as well as in the research arena. Most of these trends and challenges are being presented and discussed during this international conference on secondary education; however their application remains very limited. There is clearly a need for advocacy for a new vision of educational functions of secondary education in the 21st century.

The dilemma, academic and knowledge based education versus behavioural and life-skills education, is not a new one. It remains the subject of debate. Its origins lie in the fundamental question: is education, and more specifically secondary education, conceived and planned to satisfy the needs of society or the needs of young people? The position of this paper is that optimally it should satisfy both, as the interest of both are convergent. The right balance between knowledge based and life skills education will benefit the society as a whole.

The question now is, will we be able to meet this challenge to build a better future?

Source and Courtesy: UNESCO, Paris

Annex—D

SECONDARY EDUCATION FOR A BETTER FUTURE: TRENDS, CHALLENGES AND PRIORITIES

1. Introduction: Context, Aims and Organisation of the Conference

Context

The first article of the World Declaration on Education for All adopted by the World Conference on Education For All held in Jomtein in 1990 asserted that *"every person-child, youth and adult—shall be able to benefit from educational opportunities designed to meet their basic learning needs"*. Ten years after Jomtien, the Dakar Framework for Action (UNESCO, 2000) stated, "Education is a fundamental human right. It is the key to sustainable development and peace and stability within and among countries, and thus an indispensable means for effective participation in the societies and economies of the twenty-first century, which are affected by rapid globalisation".

Out of the six Dakar goals, three had direct implications for the development of Secondary Education. These three goals implied a massive growth of Secondary Education in order to absorb primary school completers, ensure gender parity in enrolment and provide access for all young people to appropriate learning and life skills. More specifically, the Delors, Report exhorted us to see Secondary Education "as a crucial point in the lives of individuals: it is at this stage that young people should be able to decide their own future, in the light of their own tastes and aptitudes, and that they can acquire the abilities that will make for a successful adult life".

The report continued that Secondary Education "should thus be adapted to take account both of the different processes whereby adolescents attain maturity...and of economic and social needs".

Aware of the fundamental importance of education and the growing need to focus on Secondary Education, the international community has taken up the challenge. Clear commitments have been made within the Dakar framework for action to improve the relevance and effectiveness of Secondary Education. The international conference on secondary education held between December 22 and 24, 2002 in Muscat, was another crucial step on this journey.

Conference Aims and Organisation

In order to complement international efforts and facilitate policy dialogue in respect of this commitment to Secondary Education, The Sultanate of Oman Ministry of Education International Conference on Reform of Secondary Education—"Secondary Education for a Better Future: Trends, Challenges and Priorities" — aimed to build on both the results of National Seminar on Secondary Education held in Muscat in April, 2002 and the results of the UNESCO International Expert Meeting on General Secondary Education in the 21st Century held in Beijing in May 2001.

The Oman conference received delegates from around 34 countries, contained a total of 77 presentations and was attended by over 400 participants. It was the first time that an international education conference of this magnitude had taken place in the Sultanate and arose because of, as Yahaya bin Saud bin Mansoor Al-Sulaimi, Minister of Education stressed in his opening address, "the importance of exchanging views and experiences with educators so as to enrich the educational system". Secondary Education was described by the Minister as "an important turning point and significant phase in the future of students, and played a key role in economic development and as an engine of social change. Secondary education, in particular, is at a crossroads which can lead in different directions—to specialised and academic higher education, to technical and professional education or directly to the world of work".

Similarly, His Excellence the Director General of UNESCO, Koïchiro Matsuura, in his opening remarks to the conference, pointed out that Secondary Education was of critical importance "in making our future world a better one". He stressed both Secondary Education's impact during the period of adolescence "when important life choices and career orientations for the future are made and its contribution to human resources development as linked with the broader process of social and economic development". However, the Director General of UNESCO was clear in his belief that Secondary Education needs to be redefined if it is to fulfil its assigned functions, that is "*to prepare learners in both formal and non-formal settings for higher education, the world of work and, perhaps most importantly, for responsible citizenship in a changing world*".

In order to continue the international examination of Secondary Education, the Oman conference sought to answer four major questions. These questions were built into five themes treated sequentially over the course of the three days of the conference, each by a keynote speaker and a range of between 10 to 18 refereed papers (see the Conference Programme in Annex 3). In addition, the conference was:

- His Excellency Yahya bin Saud bin Mansoor Al-Sulaimi, Minister of Education
- His Excellency Koïchiro Matsuura, Director General of UNESCO
- Dr. Said Al- Mulais, Director General of the Arab Bureau of Education for the Gulf States
- His Excellence Mohammed bin Hamdan Al-Tobi, Under-Secretary for Educational Planning and Projects in the Ministry of Education

- Dr. Aziza Banani, Moroccan Ambassador to UNESCO and Chairwomen of the UNESCO Executive Council
- A speech presented by a representative from the Islamic Organisation for Education, Science and Culture (ISESCO) (Annex 4 contains the speeches presented at the conference)

The conference themes and topics concentrated on:

(a) Redefining secondary education for the 21st century: why change is essential

(b) Effective new models for secondary education in the 21st century: the focus for change

(c) Strategies for successful implementation of reform: practical blueprints for change

(d) Practices in evaluating the success of reform

(e) Sharing new ideas for change

Outline of Report

This report of the Conference is organised around the first four of these five themes (Themes A, B, C and D). The material from Theme E, sharing new ideas, is not treated a separate theme but incorporated, as appropriate, into the other four themes. The report is heavily based on theme rapporteur reports, which, in turn, are based on issue rapporteur reports and many hours of discussion among issue, session and theme rapporteurs and Ministry of Education and UNESCO representatives.

The report will be clearer in what it has to say about the early themes, that is why and what to change then the later themes. The reason is based on the fact that as one moves through the themes they tend to become more specific. As a theme becomes more specific then the view taken in this report is that its resolution requires greater consideration of country and local considerations. This position may be disappointing for some who are looking for 'the answers' but it is consistent with the evidence on successful implementation which shows that those involved in any change need to be fully involved in its development, implementation and assessment—if for no other reason than this involvement results in greater commitment to and acceptance of responsibility for the change. Oman is one country that is clearly on the right track here, for as pointed out by the Ministry of Education, participation in current educational reform efforts has "included all stakeholders—students, parents, teachers, administrators and tertiary education representatives as well as representatives from the private sector and educationalists".

The report undertakes a comparison of outcomes from recent UNESCO reports on Secondary Education from Beijing, Bangkok, Beirut, and Mauritius with the outcomes of both the Oman national and international conferences.

The report also identifies a number of potentially competing theories, beliefs or 'tensions' that became clearer as the conference proceeded. It is argued that while these theories or beliefs are best seen as balances rather than tensions, they will need attention if Secondary Education is to be effectively developed for the 21st Century. An example of one of these balances is that between the forces of globalisation and the need to retain a local identity.

The conclusions from Oman/UNESCO conference and the comparison with the results of other reports lead to a number of clear recommendations for reforming Secondary Education. No recommendation is more important than that Secondary Education should be given higher priority—for as the World Bank has also concluded, "education, not physical capital, has become the major source of present and future wealth of nations".

2. Conference Themes

The conference themes were:

(a) Redefining secondary education for the 21st century: why change is essential

(b) Effective new models for secondary education in the 21st century: the focus for change

(c) Strategies for successful implementation of reform: practical blueprints for change

(d) Practices in evaluating the success of reform

(e) Sharing new ideas for change

In summary, the conference had the following to say about each of these themes.

Theme A: Re-defining Secondary Education for the 21st Century—Why Change is Essential

Conference papers, presentations and discussions described a rapidly changing world both within and across countries. In particular:

- rapid developments in science, medicine and technology but unevenness in their availability; and
- wide differences in population growth (for example, in Oman 60 per cent of the total population are under the age of 18).

The result of this rapidly changing world was seen to be increased complexity, for example, from:

- a blurring of boundaries (such as, from the pressures the global marketplace facilitated by developments in information communications technology);
- the end of certainty; and
- growing inequalities in and across societies (including, as a result of poverty, gender, armed conflict, or even the digital divide).

Major issues raised by this rapid change and increased complexity were seen to include:

- economic competitiveness;
- an economic and labour market where national wealth becomes increasingly knowledge-based and there are changes in the nature of employment;
- sustainability;

- identity within globalisation; and
- equity.

As UNESCO's Director General, Mr. Koïchiro Matsuura, pointed out, the global context sees peace and security threatened in many parts of the world from factors such as civil war, HIV/AIDS, poverty, wide-spread degradation of renewable resources, illiteracy, and attempts at cultural homogeneity. He goes on to state that, "*Education has a key role to play in making our future world a better one... [and that in] all these areas, Secondary Education has an important contribution to make*".

With universal Primary Education being achieved, Secondary Education was seen by a number of presenters at the conference as the weakest link of education systems, while at the same time it becomes the fastest-expanding sector of formal education. *Secondary Education has become the weakest link not only because of the low enrolment ratio and high dropout rates in some developing nations but also the low relevance, quality and efficiency of programmes, due to factors such as*:

- out-dated information-cramming, discipline-based, college-bound curriculum and an examination-driven evaluation system over-emphasising test-scores measuring cognitive achievement and entrance to university;
- passive student/teacher relations rather than ones that promote social construction of knowledge as well as cooperation, problem-solving and critical thinking (for example, in terms of desired generic work skills and/or individual and national identity in an era of globalisation);
- inadequate background (including the qualifications) of many teachers and educational managers;
- over-centralised administration;
- limited stakeholder involvement in education, including from the private sector; and

- inadequate, inappropriate and uncritical use of the multiple sources of available information, including through the new technology.

These perceived weaknesses of current Secondary Education systems are given even greater attention in a world of increased use and publication of cross-country measures of performance, such as the ongoing OECD Programme for International Student Assessment (PISA). It continues to be important, therefore, to locate national actions and strategies within an international context.

In summary, and risking over simplification, it is clear that the conference agreed that:

- secondary education should be given higher priority and that commitment to universal access to Secondary Education as an aspiration should be retained;
- change is essential and that the objectives and functions of Secondary Education need to be redefined, renewed and improved to fit with the new realities of the twenty-first century;
- despite the challenges and dilemmas that face Secondary Education now and in the future, reform must continue and build on current strength and weaknesses; and
- continued collaboration is required, both nationally and internationally, including in the provision of evidence-based information and examples of innovative best practice.

In brief, and as UNESCO's Director General, Mr. Koïchiro Matsuura, pointed out, *"a major, well-coordinated effort must...be made by national authorities, with the support of international and regional organisations and the active participation of civil society, to meet the long-term objective of universalising quality Secondary Education in the perspective of Education for All"*.

Theme B: Effective New Models for Secondary Education in the 21st Century—The Focus for Change

The analysis of context cannot merely consist in identifying over-whelming trends (Theme A) to which we must necessarily submit. Among these trends, educators have to differentiate between what is acceptable and what is not. The conference argued that children are the starting point for a strategy about the future of schooling. A constructive and optimistic vision of their futures and needs should inform the structure and processes of education. However, when the question is asked, 'Does Secondary Education achieved such a vision?" the answer is at best a confused 'perhaps' and at worst 'no'.

UNESCO's DG, Mr. Matsuura argued, "the concept of basic education [is] an evolving one: the more the world changes and the more complex societies become, the more sophisticated are the skills needed for social integration and economic participation. This broadens the scope of basic education learned in primary and secondary schools". He added that, "what is currently understood as 'basic education' will be a necessary but insufficient condition. *It can be anticipated that the changes in the twenty-first century will require the expansion, adaptation and improvement of Secondary Education, for the benefit of all"*.

The Delors Report was clear in its recommendation that *"learning in schools needs to focus not just on knowing but also doing, living together and being"*. As secondary schooling is the learning environment in which many young people negotiate their passage through adolescence towards early adulthood, life skills are of particular importance. If schools are not coping with these skills, who else will?

What should be the focus for change in secondary education? The conference papers, presentations and discussions answered this question in a reasonable consistent way. In brief, there was seen to be a need to:

- balance knowledge and cognitive skills with behavioural and like skills (including problem-solving and critical thinking);

- balance vocational and academic education as well as meet the needs of post-secondary education;
- raise the awareness of the importance of career guidance;
- increased flexibility and diversity in both content and processes, for example between formal, non-formal and distance education;
- offer students a variety of choices according to their needs, interests and potentials, but in so doing avoid overcrowding the curriculum;
- integrate technology into education; and
- develop assessment systems that have a balance among reliability, validity, practicability, and compatibility with teaching as well as being centrally and teacher produced.

In terms of curriculum models, it was recommended that *what can be learnt effectively at school may better limited to a set of generic competencies necessary for all work and applicable to a wide range of circumstances*. Such generic competencies have started to appear in recent reviews of education systems. For example, one such review resulted in four new basic clusters for organising the curriculum:

- life pathways and social futures (who am I and where am I going?);
- multiliteracies and communications media (how do I make sense of and communicate with the world?);
- active citizenship (what are my rights and responsibilities in communities, cultures and economies?); and
- environments and technologies (how do I describe, analyse and shape the world around me?).

Included under the heading of behavioural and life skills, a number of presenters argued persuasively that schools need to participate in the global agenda to transform a culture of peace. The active involvement of youth in the promotion of living together, peace, human rights, sustainable development, and international understanding was seen to need to increase markedly.

Also argued was the need to maintain the dignity of students. Dignity comes from education 'to be'. Yet many curricula and school and teacher practices were seen as marginalising student identity by ignoring their voices and choices. Students, it was argued, must be given the opportunity to express their authentic selves and discover their potentials. In this regard, the whole notion of screening, selection and shifting, especially on a very narrow set of cognitive criteria, may be obsolete. If the scope for cheap labour is continually shrinking what is the fate of those who have 'failed' in schools? Does it make economic sense for a society to have the majority of its young seeing themselves of failures?

Finally, in terms of building new curriculum models, a particular tension was reported in a number of presentations between pressures exerted by globalisation/modernity and local identity/traditions. This tension manifest itself, for example, in the balance between pressures exerted by Western modernity and keeping the modest Islamic traditions.

In summary, the conference agreed that in respect of effective models for Secondary Education in the 21st Century:

- countries continue to be committed to the goal of mass, universally accessed Secondary Education;
- there is a recognition that traditionally academically based education and the notion of screening, especially on a very narrow set of cognitive criteria, do not adequately address students' or the society's needs in a context of rapid economic, cultural and social change—schools need to focus and be assessed not just on their contributions to knowing but also to doing, living together and being;
- life skills are of particular importance—with the active involvement of youth in the promotion of living

together, peace, human rights, sustainable development, and international understanding needing to be increased markedly;

- there is a need to balance vocational/technical and academic education as well as meet the needs of post-Secondary Education;
- education systems and schools need to increase flexibility, responsiveness and diversity in both content and processes offering students a variety of choices according to their needs, interests and potentials—but at the same time not overcrowded the curriculum; and
- there is a need in all that we do to maintain student dignity.

Theme C: Strategies for Successful Implementation of Reform—Practical Blue-prints for Change

How to change (the priorities or strategies for effective implementation) was the topic of Theme C. In summary, strategies for successful implementation of reform were seen to rest on at least five pillars:

- student involvement, as well as taking account of students and their needs;
- teacher involvement, and quality of pre and ongoing in-service teacher education (and selection for);
- quality leadership, and its development and renewal;
- family and community involvement, and development (social capital); and
- private and public sector involvement, particularly in addressing labour market demands. In fact, what was suggested was a multi-sectoral approach enlisting the collective efforts of government and their ministries, NGOs, local communities, the private sector, etc.

Implicit in this vision for wide stakeholder involvement in educational reform is that successful implementation:

- favours a move from centralised to decentralised school and system management, including greater use of networking;
- takes time;
- is developmental in nature; and
- needs to recognise that people (students, teachers, principals) develop knowledge and skills on a continuing basis (lifelong learning).

Theme B (the focus for change) has already stressed the importance of students, of taking account of them and their needs, particularly in the behavioural and life skill areas. Theme B also stressed the importance of maintaining student dignity. Theme C conference papers, presentations and discussions argued for greater student involvement in school curriculum and administration. Through this involvement students were seen to need to be able to develop the confidence.

To attempt to bring about major change without carrying along teachers was seen as very unwise. Compliance without commitment, it was argued, does not bring about successful long-term implementation. Reform of schooling, no matter how well conceptualised, powerfully sponsored, or closely audited will often fail in the face of resistance (or inaction) from teachers. Teacher shortages were seen as compounding any implementation difficulties. *Given the importance of teachers in a strategy of successful implementation of reform, the quality of the criteria for their selection and their pre and in-service education become especially important as areas requiring attention*.

School leaders, including principles were also seen as critically important in achieving school effectiveness and improvement and, as reforms designed to raise standards are introduced (for example, decentralisation and school-based-management and/or community involvement), their roles change significantly.

It was argued that a new kind of educational leader is required and that policy makers should be compelled to develop and modify their national training strategies to equip school leaders with the knowledge and skills required to carry out these changed roles.

Reframing schools as learning organisations, where the structures, processes and practices foster continuous, learning of all those involved, is rapidly gaining favour in both the arenas of research and policy. The concept of schools as learning organisations has grown out of the need to create school environments where all are learning how to learn together. This development reinforces the need to distinguish between leadership as a function which all can do (that is, distributive leadership) and leadership as a role which is held by the position holder, such as the principal.

But school settings are not necessarily conducive to such learning, especially where it extends beyond the school to family and community involvement and development. This situation is unfortunate, especially given the strong link between such factors as home educational environment and school climate and results—a stronger link in some countries than socio-economic status. School councils representing all parties comprising a community with active encouragement to attend and involvement in meaningful activities was seen as one strategy for greater family and community involvement and development. On the other hand, it was recommended that more students be given opportunities to be involved in such councils as well as in community service.

Private and public sector institutions were seen as playing an important role in strategies for successful implementation of reform.

This involvement could take a number of forms, including support for infrastructure, specific projects, sponsorship, and curriculum initiatives. These private and public institutions could profitably be involved in strengthening the linkage between schools and the world of work through vocational guidance, study-work alternation and clarification of changing labour market requirements.

The general consensus, after many years of educational reform initiatives, was that too little changes too slowly. This situation is particularly so in a context where too much is implemented too quickly. Permeating all the recommendations on how to change was the position that strategies for effective implementation favour decentralised management, take time, are developmental in nature, and need to recognise that people (students, teachers, principals) develop knowledge and skills on a continuing basis (lifelong learning).

For example, research on schools as learning organisations has shown clearly that one needs to first get the personal/ interpersonal, distributive leadership, collective teacher efficacy or trusting and collaborative climate 'right'. Once the personal/ interpersonal is 'right' then it can be used to focus on the educational/instructional, including having a shared and monitored mission. Once the educational/instructional is 'right' and there is confidence in what the school is doing and why it is doing it, then the leaders and school can more to development/ learning/change, to taking initiatives and risks, including for example working with others schools in a 'nested' model.

Development implies another important principle—one needs stability for change, one needs to constantly move ahead but without losing one's roots. Put another way, one needs a base or agreed position from which to develop; one needs to stand for something, to first be 'grounded'. In targeting strategies or interventions to help this development recognition needs to be given to the fact that actions at one stage may be inappropriate, or even counterproductive, at another stage. Achieving balanced learning/development may, in fact, mean that a school system or individual school recognises and understands such stages and can take the appropriate action without being 'bowled over' by the change that surrounds it. It may mean understanding (to jump briefly to Theme D) that schools will be evaluated differently depending on the stage it has reached. It also, eventually, involves those in education systems and schools being risk takers.

Theme D: Practices in Evaluating the Success of Reform

Theme D focused on how do we know we've been successful, or the practices we might use in evaluating the success of reform. Topics considered by the conference in answering this question centred on:

- accountability;
- maximising access, opportunity and completion rates;
- measuring improvement in educational outcomes; and
- examining indicators of capacity building at the school and community level.

Accountability in education is a contested and complex concept. Despite this, some form of accountability is as inevitable as it is important. Given the growing understanding of the crucial importance of education for the future prosperity of their countries (see Theme A), it was reported that governments are looking for ways to exercising central control over schools. Part of the logic for these developments is linked to exposing education to the market.

Despite these national developments in educational accountability, there are those, usually from outside national governments and their ministries, who urge caution. There are contested areas and they seem to centre on questions such as why accountability is being undertaken (for example, for central control, resource distribution and/or local school improvement) and who and what is involved (for example, the employer, professionals, parents, and/or students and central and/or local curriculum standards, inspection, testing).

It might be that centrally-defined output criteria and local innovation in finding ways of meeting them are not necessarily contradictory; what matters is the degree to which specification of standards becomes so detailed and interventionist that a culture of control rather than autonomy develops. It was reported, for example, that the establishment of student standards, wide-spread student testing of their achievement and judgements about schools and teachers based on the results can have disastrous unintended consequences. For students, such consequences may include, minimising their individual differences, narrowing curriculum to which they are exposed, diverting enormous efforts from instruction to test preparation, and negatively influencing schools' willingness to accept students with weak academic records. The consequences for teachers may include the creation of incentives for cheating, feelings of shame, guilt and anger, and a sense of dissonance and alienation and to the atrophy of teachers' instructional repertoires.

Accountability pressures are not only national in nature. At the international level UNESCO's Monitoring Learning Achievement (MLA) project and OECD's PISA are having an impact on national educational policy. Given the cautions about some developments in educational accountability, what was thought encouraging about this international work was its taking into account such factors as the socio-economic status and home educational environment of the student, the school learning environment and a broad range of educational outcomes, including not only different literacies but also student life skills and engagement in their education.

The degree of inclusion practised in different education systems, in terms of factors such as maximising access, opportunity and completion rates, was found to vary quite widely—from including only those with special education needs to any group which might be marginalised, whether these be girls or boys, ethnic minorities and/or the gifted and talented. There was felt to be a need, for example, to raise the awareness the social, economic and development cost of neglecting the education of girls and establishing sound indicators to monitor and evaluate technical and vocational tracks offered for them. But it was agreed that there was still much to do in making schools more inclusive, including providing appropriate training for teachers, materials and equipment. Pleas were made for more time to make the required changes and more forums for exchange of experiences.

While the final aim of a school-reform evaluator must be to discover if a reform programme has led to improved educational quality, an important along-the-way choice faces those measuring improvement—do they take a 'hands-off' appraisal or, instead, take a more proactive role in nurturing improvement? Given that research are experience have shown that the tests of students' performance are immensely influential on the instruction that transpires as part of any reform initiative, it was argued that it is incumbent on the school-reform evaluator to first installs instructionally supportive tests as their dominant data-gathering device.

A major highlight in Theme D was a *call to broaden what counts for effective education beyond academic achievement to what could be termed 'capacity building'*. For example, very interesting data was reported from a British cohort study found that attentiveness in school at age 10 years was a key aspect of human capital production at age 26, also influencing female wages even taking into account qualifications. Boys with high levels of conduct disorder were much more likely to experience unemployment. High self-esteem was found to both reduce the likelihood of that unemployment lasting more than a year and, for all males, increase wages. Locus of control was an important predictor of female wages. Good peer relations were found to reduce the probability of unemployment and increasing female wages. These findings, as well as the arguments presented earlier in respect of the crucial importance of learning to learn, cooperation, problem-solving, critical thinking, and so on, add weight to those expressing concerns about the sole reliance on academic, cognitive achievement to measure success.

In summary, practices for evaluating the success of reform should understand that:

- care needs to be taken that the degree to standards specification does not become so detailed and interventionist that a culture of control rather than autonomy develops;
- there is a need to raise the awareness the social, economic and development costs of weak inclusion policies, including a neglect of girls education;

- school-reform evaluators need to first install instructionally supportive tests as their dominant data-gathering device;
- measuring educational success has to take into account such contextual factors as the socio-economic status and home educational environment of the student and the school learning environment; and
- measuring educational success has to rely on more than academic, cognitive achievement.

3. Comparison of Outcomes from UNESCO Reports from Beijing, Beirut, Bangkok, and Mauritius with the Outcomes of the Muscat National and International Conferences

A comparison of outcomes from recent UNESCO reports from meetings in Beijing, Bangkok, Beirut, and Mauritius with the outcomes of the Sultanate of Oman national and international conferences on Secondary Education, contained in the following chart, leave the one with a number of very clear impressions:

- agreement that education has a key role to play in making our future world a better one;
- consistency advice on why, what and how to change Secondary Education to achieve this better world;
- the need for greater national and international priority to be given to Secondary Education;
- the need not just for Secondary Education to be expanded but also for its objectives and functions to be redefined, renewed and improved; and
- a continuing role for international bodies such as UNESCO in facilitating dialogue and providing evidence-based information about this redefinition, renewal and improvement.

In the chart that follows, a summary of the results from the conference is used (left hand column) as the basis of comparison with the other reports. If an additional recommendation is identified it is added in the column representing that report. A summary of the outcomes of each of these reports can be found in the Annex. The reports consulted are as follows:

- UNESCO. (2001) Executive Summary: Meeting Agreements. *International Expert Meeting on General Secondary Education in the Twenty-first Century: Trends, Challenges and Priorities.* Paris: UNESCO Final Report on the meeting held in Beijing, People's Republic of China, May 21-25, pp. 5-8.
- Billeh, V. Boujaoude, S., and Sulieman, S. (2002). *Regional Synthesis on Development of Secondary Education in the Arab States.* Beirut: UNESCO Regional Office.
- Zhou Nan-zhao and Haw, G. (2002). *Secondary Education Reforms in Asia-Pacific Region: Challenges, Strategies and Programme Actions in Addressing Learners' Needs.* A report on the 8th UNESCO-APEID International Conference in Education held in Bangkok 26-29 November, 2002 and presented as a paper at Sultanate of Oman Ministry of Education/UNESCO International Conference Secondary Education for a Better Future: Trends, Challenges and Priorities, Muscat, Sultanate on Oman, 22-24 December. (2002). pp. 19-22.
- UNESCO Dakar Regional Office, (2002). *General Report of the Regional Workshop on the Reform of Secondary Education in Africa.* Mauritius, 3-6 December, 2002.
- Sultanate of Oman/Ministry of Education, *Recommendations of the National Seminar on Secondary Education. Muscat, 1-3 April 2002.*

Comparison of Outcomes from UNESCO Reports and Oman

	Muscat Oman / UNESCO 01/12/2002	*Beijing UNESCO May 02*	*Beirut UNESCO December 02*	*Mauritius UNESCO December 02*	*Bangkok UNESCO November 02*	*Muscat OMAN April 02*
1.	**Why Change?**					
1.1	Secondary Education should be given higher priority and that commitment to universal access to Secondary Education as an aspiration should be retained.	X	I	I	X	I
1.2	change is essential and that the objectives and functions of Secondary Education need to be redefined, renewed and improved to fit with the new realities of the twenty-first century;	X	I	I	X	I
1.3	despite the challenges and dilemmas that face secondary education now and in the future, reform must continue and build on current strengths and weaknesses; and,	X		X	I	I
1.4	1.4 continued collaboration is required, both nationally and internationally, including in the provision of evidence-based information and examples of innovative best practice.	X	X	X	X	X
		I			Major review (like Jomtien)	

(Contd...)

	Muscat Oman / UNESCO 01/12/2002	Beijing UNESCO May 02	Beirut UNESCO December 02	Mauritius UNESCO December 02	Bangkok UNESCO November 02	Muscat OMAN April 02
2	**What Change?**					
2.1	countries continue to be committed to the goal of mass, universally accessed Secondary Education;	X		I	I	I
2.2	there is a recognition that, traditionally academically based education and the notion of screening, especially on a very narrow set of cognitive criteria, do not adequately address students? or the society's needs in a context of rapid economic, cultural and social change—schools need to focus and be assessed not just on their contributions to knowing but also to doing, living together and being;	X	X	X	X	X
2.3	life skills are of particular importance—with the active involvement of youth in the promotion of living together, peace, human rights, sustainable development, and international understanding needing to be increased markedly;	X		X	X	X
2.4	there is a need to balance vocational/technical and academic education as well as meet the needs of post-Secondary Education;	X	X	X	X	X

(Contd...)

	Muscat Oman / UNESCO 01/12/2002	*Beijing UNESCO May 02*	*Beirut UNESCO December 02*	*Mauritius UNESCO December 02*	*Bangkok UNESCO November 02*	*Muscat OMAN April 02*
2.5	education systems and schools need to increase flexibility, responsiveness and diversity in both content and processes–offering students a variety of choices according to their needs, interests and potentials—but at the same time not overcrowd the curriculum; and	X	X	X	X	X
2.6	there is a need in all that we do to maintain student dignity.	I		I	X	I
		X		X	Creative use of ICT	X
						Islamic ideology and Oman cultural identity will be the base for reform
						Increasing learning time in school day and year

(Contd…)

Muscat Oman/UNESCO 01/12/2002	Beijing UNESCO May 02	Beirut UNESCO December 02	Mauritius UNESCO December 02	Bangkok UNESCO November 02	Muscat OMAN April 02
3. How Change?					
3.1 student involvement, as well as taking account of students and their needs;	X	X	X	X	I
3.2 teacher involvement, and quality pre and on going in-service teacher education (including selection for);	X	X	X	X	X
3.3 quality leadership, and its development and renewal;	X		X Including capacity building		X
3.4 family and community involvement, and development (social capital);	X	X	X	X	I
3.5 private and public sector involvement, particularly in addressing labour market demands. In fact, what is suggested is a multi-sectoral approach enlisting the collective efforts of government and their ministries, NGOs, local communities, the private sector, etc.	X	X	X	X	X
3.6 move from centralised to decentralised school and system management including greater participation of all stakeholders and use of networking;	X	X	X	X	X
3.7 take time;					

(Contd...)

	Muscat Oman/UNESCO 01/12/2002	Beijing UNESCO May 02	Beirut UNESCO December 02	Mauritius UNESCO December 02	Bangkok UNESCO November 02	Muscat OMAN April 02
3.8	see change as developmental in nature; and			I		
3.9	recognise that people (students, teachers, principals) develop knowledge and skills on a continuing basis (lifelong learning)	X	X	I		
		Student should be the centre of reform		X		
				Adequate infrastructure situated close to clients		Decrease emphasis on text books Establish regional teacher training centres
4	**How do we know we've been successful?**					
4.1	care needs to be taken that the degree of standards specification does not become so detailed and interventionist that a culture of control rather than autonomy develops;			X		
4.2	there is a need to raise the awareness the social economic and development cost of weak inclusion policies including a neglect of girls' education;	X		I		

(Contd...)

Muscat Oman/UNESCO 01/12/2002	*Beijing UNESCO May 02*	*Beirut UNESCO December 02*	*Mauritius UNESCO December 02*	*Bangkok UNESCO November 02*	*Muscat OMAN April 02*
4.3 school-reform evaluators need to first install instructionally supportive tests as their dominant data-gathering device;			X		I
4.4 measuring educational success has to take into account such contextual factors as the socio-economic status and home educational environment of the student and the school learning environment; and,	I		I		
4.5 measuring educational success has to rely or more than academic, cognitive achievement.	X		I	X	X
			X And use for quality control in a decentralised system	Develop core quality indicators	
	X		X	School physical and psychological health	X
	X		X	Government priority in planning	X

(Contd...)

Muscat Oman / UNESCO 01/12/2002	*Beijing UNESCO May 02*	*Beirut UNESCO December 02*	*Mauritius UNESCO December 02*	*Bangkok UNESCO November 02*	*Muscat OMAN April 02*
			X		Use continuous evaluation Establish and education and assessment centre
	Key	X = Agreement	I = Implied Agreement		

4. The Need for Balance

An overview of the different papers and the results of the various discussion sessions of the conference suggests that there was a consensus among most countries and speakers that Secondary Education is and will remain the responsibility of all stakeholders in any society and that issues surrounding Secondary Education vary according to the various social contexts but that it will need to be reformed to meet the demands of a better future.

At a macro level, the interests of each stakeholder could result in a major differences in beliefs about the definition and purpose of, and the changes needed in, Secondary Education. However, as a result of better understanding ongoing social, political and cultural changes within countries and around the world, the conference emphasised the importance of achieving balance between these interests, beliefs or 'tensions'. It is, in fact, proposed that we examine these interests or beliefs as balances rather than tensions. Focussing on different interests, beliefs or tensions might imply that we are only dealing with mutually exclusive options.

A re-examination of the results of the conference across the four Themes helps identify a number of balances. This section of the conference report provides a brief account of twelve balances—balances that, while not without overlap, might need to be 'balanced' in each education system within the general framework of developing world class Secondary Education for a better future. These balances are between:

- continuity and change;
- dependence and independence;
- individual and community;
- homogeneity and heterogeneity;
- spiritual and material;
- global and local;
- education for education and education for work as well as academic and life skills;

- competition and cooperation;
- knowledge-experience explosion and human capacity;
- uncertainty and future scenarios;
- process and outcomes; and
- social institution's expectations and educator's practices.

Continuity and Constant Change

In contrast to past continuity, recent times have witnessed constant change, a stream of new movements, new programmes and new directions. Unfortunately, conference papers give the impression that some in education seem to be forever rushing to catch the next bandwagon that hits the scene. 'Unfortunately' because there is increasing evidence that some schools and school systems have been badly disillusioned by the galloping hoof beats of the itinerant peddlers behind the new movements who ride in and out again extorting their latest elixir.

The core paradox in a such a situation, a world of massive and constant change, seems to be how to foster enough internal stability in people and the organisation in which they work in order to encourage the pursuit of change. *Stability for change, moving ahead without losing our roots, is the challenge*. Another way of putting this would be to assert that the most successful secondary schools of the new age will be those that are able to balance the market pressures of adaptation and dynamism with social concerns of security and dignity.

It might be helpful in this situation for us to remember Noah's principle: one survives not by predicting rain but by building arks. As some of the conference papers demonstrated, amid uncertain, continually changing conditions, leading educational leaders are constructing arks comprising their collective capacity to learn, they are striving to become intelligent, or learning, organisations.

Dependence and Independence

A second fundamental issue relates to the balance between dependence and independence. This situation is most easily seen conference papers implying an over dependence by those in educational institutions on 'leaders', often engendered by the overconfidence of 'leaders' in their own abilities or importance. There seem to be a lot of people around these days who want to tell those in schools what to do. This situation is unfortunate. It is unfortunate because some of those doing the telling do not always accept responsibility for their advice, are not around long enough to take responsibility for their directions and to may even seek to prevent fair and open assessment of the changes they promulgate. It is also unfortunate because while those in schools cannot avoid change they are the people who have to implement change. As some of the conference papers argued, those in schools need to have more to say about what is happening in our world, what it means for our schools and how it will be implemented and assessed—in other words, they need more independence.

Individualism and Community

It may be unreasonable to accept the schools to pickup the slack when, as described in different conference papers, families fall apart, religious institutions no longer attract the young, children are malnourished, drug addiction is rampant, prime-time television programmes are vacuous and educationally bankrupt, and gang members, athletes, and narcissistic celebrities are the admired adolescent role models. However, *if the home and school do not pick up the responsibility for our young then who will?*

Who will counter, for example, the pressure inherent in much of our 'modern' society to act alone rather than with, or for, the community? *An elementary level of trust necessary is for community. Where is such trust established, if not in our homes and schools?* Turning back the tide of a 'virtual' world, with its stress on individualism and encouragement to dissociate oneself from an increasingly challenging world, is vital for the future survival of our societies. *Community is a place where conflict can be resolved without physical or emotional bloodshed. It could be said that a community is a group that can 'fight gracefully'.*

Homogeneity and Heterogeneity

If you look for common denominators is successful institutions, it was argued that a strong one is to find a way to get some of the people to do a deviant thing, to take the initiative, to take risks. If a system is too tight for this there will be no search and no development. Also, as some conference papers pointed out, *the worker sought in the future will be one who thinks, questions, innovates and takes entrepreneurial risk, as well as one that can work in regularly changing teams.*

One lesson here is that reductionist approaches in education, to the complexity that is the world of the teacher and the student, should not go unchallenged. As a number of conference papers pointed out, uniformity for education systems in aims, in standards, and in methods of assessment is a complexity-reducing mechanism. *It is far tidier to have a single set of aims for all, a single curriculum for all, a single set of standards for all, and a single array of tests for all than to have locally developed approaches to school improvement.* However, homogeneity o^ outcome for the future of our society is not necessarily th' nighest good, and may be impossible to achieve. On the other nand, recognising diversity and acknowledging the multiple ways to be an act can be seen as a potential source of strength to a culture.

Spiritual and Material

As pointed to by the Director-General of the UNESCO during the conference opening ceremony "peace and security are threatened in many parts of the world and many countries are living in situations of crisis and conflict. Civil wars are a key source of human suffering in today's world, where billions of dollars are spent on weapons". In addition it was reported at the conference that poverty and diseases such as HIV/AIDS continues to affect millions of people, especially young people, around the world. Similarly, WHO in its recent world report on violence and health states that today no country or community is untouched by violence. Images and accounts of violence pervade the media; it is on our streets, in our homes, schools, work-places and institutions. Violence is a universal scourge that tears at the fabric of communities and threatens the life, health and happiness of all of us. Each year, more than 1.6 million people worldwide lose their lives to violence.

These horrifying facts about violence may be partly a result of the imbalance between the spiritual and the material dimensions of the human life. Therefore, it is not surprising to find a call in the conference for serious consideration of balancing human spiritual aspects and the technical productivity-based aspects in developing Secondary Education for a better future. This balance is also clearly expressed in the first of 39 recommendations from the Oman National seminar on Secondary Education held in Muscat in April, 2002: "Islamic ideology, values of the society and the Omani cultural identity shall be the base for the reform of Education in the Sultanate of Oman".

Global and Local

With the revolution of technology and telecommunications, globalisation in its various forms is a fact of today's and future life. As some conference papers argued, this does not necessarily mean the domination of one particular culture over another; rather it means people around the world being able within their respective cultures to enjoy the privilege of living together in the global village. It was seen that for this to happen a balance needed to be achieved in Secondary Education between *emphasising the role of students as citizens of their respective countries and their role as global citizens*. Related to this position was the notion of keeping balance between responding to modernity and preserving national identities.

Education for Education and Education for Work as well as Academic and Life Skills

Debate on education for its own sake or for work continued at the conference. Conference papers confirmed that *ignorance and social breakdown are not less serious than unemployment and coping with the rapidly changing job markets of the world.* Both need to be addressed. Thus, an over-emphasis on academic based education such as found in science and technology-based subjects at the expense of humanities and life-skills in secondary schools would create imbalance. The conference, in fact, concluded that *life skills are of particular importance with the active involvement of youth in the promotion of living together, peace, human rights, sustainable development, and international understanding needing to be markedly increased in secondary schools.*

Competition and Cooperation

It was reported at the conference that competitiveness permeates many education systems around the world. Nations attempt to develop human resources that are capable of competing with other nations, communities, organisations and people in various fields of life. However, nations, communities, organisations and people also cooperate and work together in order to achieve better futures. *Organisations and commercial and industrial firms, for example, and increasingly moving towards coordinating their businesses. This situation puts Secondary Education in the forefront of the challenge of educating students in both how to compete and how to cooperate.* Balance between these two concepts becomes increasingly essential in today's world.

Knowledge-experience Explosion and Human Capacity

It was reported at the conference that the quantity of the information in increasing at a staggering rate, in part due to the sheer amount of computing power available, and in part to the general explosion of knowledge and research. Thousands of publications are published daily around the world in various fields of life that report knowledge needing to be available to Secondary Education students. However, it was also argued that schools neither have time and ability during schooling years to transfer all that information to *students nor have social responsibility for doing so. Instead, some conference papers argued that students need to be taught processes for dealing with and to handle the steadily increasing amount of information and experiences to which they are exposed through the various types of media.*

The conference highlighted the significance of maintaining balance between, on one hand, the amount and the depth of information included in Secondary Education curriculum and, on the other hand, the strategies, skills and techniques that are likely to help students handle information and deal with it effectively and efficiently.

Uncertainty and Future Scenarios

Conference papers described Secondary Education today as being developed in a world increasingly characterised by great uncertainties—uncertainties associated with rapid economic, technological, political and social changes. When change accelerates, it becomes very difficult to anticipate what will occur. Some experts suggest that change has so accelerated that long-range planning is no longer possible. At the same time, participants of the conference pointed to the fact that there is a fashionable trend now-a-days to develop scenarios for the future. Educational systems attempt to develop curricula that are directed towards one of those scenarios, whether at micro or macro level. However, because of the unpredictable nature of social change there are no guarantees that the future will be as perceived in those scenarios. *It is, therefore, important to maintain balance between future expectations and curricula design through ensuring a degree of flexibility, which can make curricula constantly adaptable to changing circumstances.*

Process and Outcome

Some conference papers argue that the general direction of the debate over Secondary Education is dominated by an exaggerated emphasis on the outcomes of secondary schools without an equal emphasis placed upon the processes of preparing those outcomes. It was suggested that this imbalance is a direct, result of the overwhelming market place debate that has been going on since the 1970s. Societies (governments, politicians, parents, and even students) are concerned about what kind of skills and competencies young people will have when they graduate from secondary schools. While this concern has to be taken into account, conference papers also pointed out that it is important to be concern about the quality of processes that are responsible for creating and shaping secondary school students during the schooling years. These processes include such issues as curricula design, pedagogy, learning strategies, assessment strategies, and so on. *Balance is needed then between the development of our understanding of the kind of school graduates we need and the development of the quality of processes needed for arriving at those graduates.*

Social Institutions' Expectations and Educators' Practices

Conference papers revealed that various social institutions such as family and job market have certain expectations of secondary school graduates. Nevertheless, educators' practices in schools are not always seen to be consistent with those expectations. As a result, poor school-home and school-job market relationship are reported.

This is neither to argue for family and job market nor to argue for educators and their practices. Rather, it is to argue that effective and productive communication is needed between the various social institutions on one hand, and educators on the other. Students spend a small proportion of their time in schools and the rest outside school. *It was argued that students do better in schools when they have strong home educational environments* (including getting effective instructions from their families about how they should organise their learning time, develop plans, and create visions about their schools and life generally). Thus, it is crucial to maintain balance between what social institutions expect of students and how educators conduct teaching and learning in secondary schools.

5. Conclusions: Recommendations for Reforming Secondary Education

The Oman Ministry of Education/UNESCO International Conference on the Reform of Secondary Education, "Secondary Education for a Better Future-Trends, Challenges and Priorities", results in the following recommendations for reforming Secondary Education (recommendations marked with as asterisk are taken from material reviewed for this report from other UNESCO or Omani reports. Recommendations are organised by conference Themes.

1. *Redefining Secondary Education for the 21st Century: Why Change is Essential?*

- ❑ Secondary Education should be given higher priority and that commitment to universal access to Secondary Education as an aspiration should be retained;
- ❑ change is essential and that the objectives and functions of Secondary Education need to be redefined, renewed and improved to fit with the new realities of the twenty-first century;
- ❑ despite the challenges and dilemmas that face secondary education now and in the future, reform must continue and build on current strengths and weaknesses;
- ❑ continued collaboration is required, both nationally and internationally, including in the provision of evidence-based information and examples of innovative best practice; and
- ❑ *UNESCO undertakes a major review of Secondary Education (like Jomtien).

2. *Effective New Models for Secondary Education in the 21st Century: the Focus for Change*

- ❑ countries continue to be committed to the goal of mass, universally accessed Secondary Education;
- ❑ *the beliefs and values of the society and cultural identity need to form the base for any reform;
- ❑ there is a recognition that traditionally academically based education and the notion of screening, especially on a very narrow set of cognitive criteria, do not adequately address students' or the society's needs in a context of rapid economic, cultural and social change-schools need to focus and be assessed not just on their contributions to knowing but also to dong, living together and being;
- ❑ life skills are of particular importance—with the active involvement of youth in the promotion of living

together, peace, human rights, sustainable development, and international understanding needing to be increased markedly;

- there is a need to balance vocational/technical and academic education as well as meet the needs of post-Secondary Education;
- education systems and schools need to increase flexibility, responsiveness and diversity in both content and processes—offering students a variety of choices according to their needs, interests and potentials—but at the same time not overcrowded the curriculum (* and decrease emphasis on textbooks);
- there is a need in all that we do not maintain student dignity; and
- there is a need to better integrate and make more creative use of ICT.

3. *Strategies for Successful Implementation of Reform: Practical Blueprints for Change*

- student involvement, as well as taking account of students and their needs (students need to be the centre of any reform);
- teacher involvement, and quality pre and ongoing in-service teacher education (and selection for);
- quality leadership, and its development and renewal;
- family and community involvement and development (that is, social capital development);
- private and public sector involvement, particularly in addressing labour market demands in fact, what is suggested is a multi-sectoral approach enlisting the collective efforts of government and their ministries, NGOs, local communities, the private sector, etc.;
- move from centralised to decentralised school and system management, including greater participation of all stakeholders and use of networking;

- ❑ take time;
- ❑ see change as development in nature;
- ❑ recognise and act on the understanding that people (students, teachers, principals) develop knowledge and skills on a continuing basis (lifelong learning); and,
- ❑ recognise and act on the understanding that effective change will need to involve achieving a balance between:
  - — continuity and change;
  - — dependence and independence;
  - — individual and community;
  - — homogeneity and heterogeneity;
  - — spiritual and material;
  - — global and local;
  - — education for education and education for work as well as academic and life skills;
  - — competition and cooperation;
  - — knowledge-experience explosion and human capacity;
  - — uncertainty and future scenarios;
  - — process and outcomes; and
  - — social institution's expectations and educator's practices.

4. *Practices in Evaluating the Success of Reform*

- ❑ the level of UNESCO and Government priority in planning and resource distribution for Secondary Education;
- ❑ develop and use core quality indicators (including of school physical and psychological health);
- ❑ in measuring success a number of factors need to be taken into account, including:

- — measuring educational success has to rely on more than academic, cognitive achievement;
- — school-reform evaluators need to first install instructionally supportive tests as their dominant data-gathering device;
- — care needs to be taken that the degree of standards specification does not become so detailed and interventionist that a culture of control rather than autonomy develops;
- — measuring educational success has to take into account such contextual factors as the socio-economic status and home educational environment of the student and the school learning environment; and
- — the need to raise the awareness the social, economic and development cost of weak inclusion policies, including a neglect of girls' education.

Report of the International Conference on the Reform of Secondary Education, 22-24 December 2002, Muscat.

Courtesy: Ministry of Education, Sultanate of Oman, Muscat.
Source: UNESCO, Paris.

Bibliography

Bahri, S. 2001. *General Secondary Education in the Twenty-first Century: Trends, Challenge and Priorities*. Paris: UNESCO.

Chinapah, V. 1997. Handbook on Monitoring Learning Achievement: Towards Capacity Building. Paris: UNESCO.

Delors, J. 1996. *Learning: The Treasure* Within. Paris: UNESCO.

Fouilhoux, M. (2002). *The Situation of Secondary Level Teachers and Educational Staff: A Discussion Paper,* presented at the International Consultative Group on Secondary Education Reform and Youth Affairs, March 2002. Paris. UNESCO.

Kriegel, B. 2000. *L'éducation et l'instruction*. Entretiens Nathan. Paris: Nathan.

Leclercq, J.M. 2001. General Secondary Education in the Twenty-first Century: Trends, Challenge and Priorities. UNESCO Working Document for the Beijing International Expert Meeting on General Secondary Education.

Meirieu, P. 1998. *Quels Savoirs Enseigner dans les lycées*? Rapport de la Consultation nationale des lycéens. Paris: Ministère de l'éducation nationale.

Mulford, B and Silins, H. 2001. *Leadership for Organisational Learning and Improved Student Outcomes—What Do We Know*? NSIN Research Matters. 2001.

OECD, 2001. *Knowledge and Skills for Life. First Results the OCDE Programme for International Student Assessment (PISA) 2000*. Paris: OECD.

UNESCO. 2000. *The Dakar Framework for Action. Education for All: Meeting Our Collective Commitments*. Text Adopted by the World Education Forum, Dakar, Senegal, 26-28 April. Paris: UNESCO.

Source and Courtesy: UNESCO, Paris.

Additional Reading

Bhaskara Rao, Digumarti (1994). *Scientific Aptitude*, New Delhi: Ashish Publishing House. ISBN 81-7024-658-X.

Bhaskara Rao, Digumarti (1995). *Animal Kingdom*. New Delhi: Discovery Publishing House. ISBN 81-7141-274-2.

Bhaskara Rao, Digumarti (1995). *Batracology*. New Delhi: Discovery Publishing House. ISBN 81-7141-279-3.

Bhaskara Rao, Digumarti (1997). *Scientific Attitude*. New Delhi: Discovery Publishing House. ISBN 81-7141-381-1.

Bhaskara Rao, Digumarti (1996). *Scientific Attitude vis-à-vis Scientific Aptitude*. New Delhi: Discovery Publishing House. ISBN 81-7141-308-0.

Bhaskara Rao, Digumarti (1996). *Scientific Attitude, Scientific Aptitude and Achievement*, New Delhi: Discovery Publishing House.

Bhaskara Rao, Digumarti, Editor (1996). *Encyclopaedia of Education for All,* 5 Volumes. New Delhi: APH Publishing Corporation. ISBN 81-7024-759-4 (set).

Vol. I *Education for All: The World Conference*. ISBN 81-7024-760-8.

Vol. II *Education for All: The EPA-9 Summit*. ISBN 81-7024-761-6.

Vol. III *Education for All: Quality Education for All*. ISBN 81-7024-762-6.

Vol. IV *Education for All: Planning and Monitoring.* ISBN 81-7024-763-4.

Vol. V *Education for All: The Indian Scenario.* ISBN 81-7024-764-0.

Bhaskara Rao, Digumarti, Editor (1996). *Global Perceptions on Peace Education,* 3 Volumes. New Delhi: Discovery Publishing House. ISBN 81-7141-319-6.

Bhaskara Rao, Digumarti, Editor (1996). *National Policy on Education.* 2 Volumes. New Delhi: Anmol Publications Pvt. Ltd. ISBN 81-7488-323-1.

Bhaskara Rao, Digumarti, Editor (1997). *Care the Child,* 2 Volumes. New Delhi: Discovery Publishing House. ISBN 81-7141-394-3.

Bhaskara Rao, Digumarti, Editor (1997). *Education for the 21st Century.* New Delhi: Discovery Publishing House. ISBN 81-7141-389-7.

Bhaskara Rao, Digumarti, Editor (1997). *Reflections on Scientific Attitude.* New Delhi: Discovery Publishing House, ISBN 81-7141-319-6.

Bhaskara Rao, Digumarti, Editor (1997). *Success Story of a Primary Education Project.* New Delhi: APH Publishing Corporation. ISBN 81-7024-850-7.

Bhaskara Rao, Digumarti, Editor (1997). *World Food Summit.* New Delhi: Discovery Publishing House. ISBN 81-7141-386-2.

Bhaskara Rao, Digumarti, Editor (1998). *Adolescence Education.* New Delhi: Discovery Publishing House. ISBN 81-7141-432-X.

Bhaskara Rao, Digumarti, Editor (1998). *Community and School Nutrition Education.* New Delhi: Discovery Publishing House. ISBN 81-7141-435-4.

Bhaskara Rao, Digumarti, Editor (1998). *District Primary Education Programme.* New Delhi: Discovery Publishing House. ISBN 81-7141-396-X.

Bhaskara Rao, Digumarti, Editor (1998). *Earth Summit,* 2 Volumes. New Delhi: Discovery Publishing House. ISBN 81-7141-435-4.

Bhaskara Rao, Digumarti, Editor (1998). *National Policy on Education: Towards an Enlightened and Humane Society*, New Delhi: Discovery Publishing House. ISBN 81-7141-426-5.

Bhaskara Rao, Digumarti, Editor (1998). *Reforming School Education*. New Delhi: Discovery Publishing House. ISBN 81-7141-403-6.

Bhaskara Rao, Digumarti, Editor (1998). *Teacher Education in India*. New Delhi: Discovery Publishing House. ISBN 81-7141-406-0.

Bhaskara Rao, Digumarti, Editor (1998). *World Summit for Social Development*. New Delhi: Discovery Publishing House. ISBN 81-7141-420-6.

Bhaskara Rao, Digumarti, Editor (2000). *Education for All: Achieving the Goal*, 3 Volumes, New Delhi: APH Publishing Corporation. ISBN 81-7648-152-1.(Set)

Vol. I *The Global Consensus*. ISBN 81-7648-155-6.

Vol. II *Mid-Decade Review Reports of Regional Seminars*. ISBN 81-7648-154-8.

Vol. III *Issues and Trends*. ISBN 81-7648-155-6.

Bhaskara Rao, Digumarti, Editor (1999), *International Encyclopaedia of AIDS*, 11 Volumes in 13 Parts. New Delhi: Discovery Publishing House. ISBN 81-7141-6 (Set).

Vol. 1 *Introduction to HIV / AIDS*. ISBN 81-7141-523-7.

Vol. 2 *HIV / AIDS—Issues and Challenges*, 2 Parts. ISBN 81-7141-524-5.

Vol. 3 *HIV / AIDS—Socio Economic Realities*. ISBN 81-7141-524-3.

Vol. 4 *HIV / AIDS—Law Ethics and Human Rights*, 2 Parts. ISBN 81-7141-526-1.

Vol. 5 *AIDS and NGOs*. ISBN 81-7141-527-X.

Vol. 6 *AIDS and Home Care*. ISBN 81-7141-528-8.

Vol. 7 *STD Case Management*. ISBN 81-7141-529-6.

Vol. 8 *HIV/AIDS Prevention and Care—Teaching Modules for Nurses and Midwives*. ISBN 81-7141-530-X.

Vol. 9 *HIV Prevention Education for Education for Educational Institutions*. ISBN 81-7141-531-8.

Vol. 10 *Instructional Modules for AIDS Education*. ISBN 81-7141-532-6.

Vol. 11 *School Health Education to Prevent AIDS and STD—A Package for Curriculum Planners*. ISBN 81-7141-5338-4.

Bhaskara Rao, Digumarti, Editor (2000). *International Encyclopaedia of Science and Technology Education*, 11 Volumes. New Delhi: Discovery Publishing House. ISBN 81-7141-548-2 (Set).

Vol. 1 *Science and Technology Education*. ISBN 81-7141-568-7.

Vol. 2 *Science Education in Developing Countries*. ISBN 81-7141-570-9.

Vol. 3 *Organisational Structure of Science*. ISBN 81-7141-570-9.

Vol. 4 *Science Education in Asia and the Pacific*. ISBN 81-7141-571-7.

Vol. 5 *Science and Technology Education for All*. ISBN 81-7141-572-5.

Vol. 6 *Values, Ethics, Talent and Girls in Science and Technology Education*. ISBN 81-7141-573-3.

Vol. 7 *Popularization of Science and Technology Education*. ISBN 81-7141-574-1.

Vol. 8 *Science, Power and Society*. ISBN 81-7141-575-X.

Vol. 9 *Information Technology*. ISBN 81-7141-576-8.

Vol. 10 *Teacher Training in Science and Technology Education*. ISBN 81-7141-577-6.

Vol. 11 *Teacher Training in Science and Technology: A Curriculum Framework*. ISBN 81-7141-578-4.

Bhaskara Rao, Digumarti, Editor (2001). *Distance Education in Different Countries*. New Delhi: APH Publishing Corporation. ISBN 81-7648-229-3.

Bhaskara Rao, Digumarti, Editor (2001). *Decentralised Management of Education (Management of Education in Panchayati Raj and Municipal Bodies)*. New Delhi: Discovery Publishing House. ISBN 81-7141-617-9.

Bhaskara Rao, Digumarti, Editor (2001). *Electrochemistry for Environmental Protection*. New Delhi: Discovery Publishing House. ISBN 81-7141-619-5.

Bhaskara Rao, Digumarti, Editor (2001). *Global Educational Studies*. New Delhi: Discovery Publishing House. ISBN 81-7141-616-0.

Bhaskara Rao, Digumarti, Editor (2001). *Global Synthesis of Educational Assessment*. New Delhi: Discovery Publishing House. ISBN 81-7141-613-6.

Bhaskara Rao, Digumarti, Editor (2000). *International Encyclopaedia of Human Rights*. 7 Volumes in 13 Parts. New Delhi: Discovery Publishing House. (Royal Size). ISBN 81-7141-567-9 (Set).

Vol. 1 *International Instruments of Human Rights*, 2 Parts. ISBN 81-7141-595-4.

Vol. 2 *Regional Instruments of Human Rights*. ISBN 81-7141-604-7.

Vol. 3 *Human Rights and the United Nations*, 2 Parts. ISBN 81-7141-605-5.

Vol. 4 *Fact Files of Human Rights*, 3 Parts. ISBN 81-7141-605-3.

Vol. 5 *Study Stories of Human Rights*, 3 Parts. ISBN 81-7141-607-3.

Vol. 6 *International Meetings on Human Rights*, 2 Parts. ISBN 81-7141-608-X.

Vol. 7 *Professional Training in Human Rights*. ISBN 81-7141-609-8.

Bhaskara Rao, Digumarti, Editor (2001). *Jomtein Decade of Education*. New Delhi: Discovery Publishing House. ISBN 81-7141-618-7.

Bhaskara Rao, Digumarti, Editor (2001). *Nuclear Materials: Issues and Concerns*, 2 Volumes. New Delhi: Discovery Publishing House. ISBN 81-7141-611-X.

Bhaskara Rao, Digumarti, Editor (2001). *World Conference on Education for All*. New Delhi: APH Publishing Corporation. ISBN 81-7648-274-9.

Bhaskara Rao, Digumarti, Editor (2001). *World Conference on Higher Education*, New Delhi: Discovery Publishing House. ISBN 81-7141-610-1.

Bhaskara Rao, Digumarti, Editor (2001). *World Conference on Science*. New Delhi: Discovery Publishing House. ISBN 81-7141-612-8.

Bhaskara Rao, Digumarti, Editor (2003). *Inspiring Experience in Teacher Education*. New Delhi: Discovery Publishing House. ISBN 81-7141-656-X.

Bhaskara Rao, Digumarti, Editor (2003). *International Studies in Education*, 3 Volumes, New Delhi: Discovery Publishing House. ISBN 81-7141-647-0.

Bhaskara Rao, Digumarti, Editor (2003). *Military Conversion: Impact on Science and Technology*, New Delhi: Discovery Publishing House. ISBN 81-7141-578-4.

Bhaskara Rao, Digumarti, Editor (2003). *United Nations Millennium Summit*. New Delhi: Discovery Publishing House. ISBN 81-7141-632-2.

Bhaskara Rao, Digumarti, Editor (2003). *World Assembly on Aging*. New Delhi: Discovery Publishing House. ISBN 81-7141-637-3.

Bhaskara Rao, Digumarti, Editor (2003). *World Conference on Human Rights*. New Delhi: Discovery Publishing House. ISBN 81-7141-661-6.

Bhaskara Rao, Digumarti, Editor (2003). *World Education Forum*. New Delhi: Discovery Publishing House. ISBN 81-7141-639-X.

Bhaskara Rao, Digumarti, Editor (2003). *Education Employment and Human Resource Development*. New Delhi: Discovery Publishing House. ISBN 81-7141-681-0.

Bhaskara Rao, Digumarti, Editor (2003). *Successful Schooling*. New Delhi: Discovery Publishing House. ISBN 81-7141-677-2.

Bhaskara Rao, Digumarti, Editor (2003). *European Education and Teachers*. New Delhi: Discovery Publishing House. ISBN 81-7141-702-7.

Bhaskara Rao, Digumarti, Editor (2003). *Teachers in a Changing World*. New Delhi: Discovery Publishing House. ISBN 81-7141-694-2.

Bhaskara Rao, Digumarti, Editor (2004). *Learning to Live Together*, 4 Volumes. New Delhi: Discovery Publishing House.

Vol. 1 *International Conference on Learning to Live Together.*

Vol. 2 *Globalisation and Living Together.*

Vol. 3 *Curriculum for Learning to Live Together.*

Vol. 4 *Science Education for the Contemporary Society.*

Bhaskara Rao, Digumarti, Editor (2004). *International Guidelines on Open and Distance Teacher Education*. New Delhi: Discovery Publishing House.

Bhaskara Rao, Digumarti, Editor (2004). *Reforming Secondary Education*. New Delhi: Discovery Publishing House.

Bhaskara Rao, Digumarti, Editor (2004). *Lifelong Learning in the 21st Century*. New Delhi: Discovery Publishing House.

Bhaskara Rao Digumarti, Editor (2004). *Adult Learning in the 21st Century*. New Delhi: Discovery Publishing House.

Bhaskara Rao, Digumarti, Editor (2004). *General Secondary Education in the 21st Century. New Delhi: Discovery Publishing House.*

Bhaskara Rao, Digumarti, Editor (2004). *Educational Practices: Research and Recommendations*. New Delhi: Discovery Publishing House.

Bhaskara Rao, Digumarti, Editor (2004). *Human Rights Education*, New Delhi. Discovery Publishing House.

Bhaskara Rao, Digumarti, Editor (2004). *United Nations Decade for Human Rights Education*. New Delhi: Discovery Publishing House.

Bhaskara Rao, Digumarti, C.A.P. Swami and B.S.V. Dutt (1997). *Self-Evaluation in Student Teaching*. New Delhi: Discovery Publishing House. ISBN 81-7141-374-9.

Bhaskara Rao, Digumarti, Editor (2003). *Education: Programmesand Policies*. New Delhi: APH Publishing Corporation. ISBN 81-7648-470-9.

Bhaskara Rao, Digumarti and D. Naresh Kumar (2004). *School Teacher Effectiveness*. New Delhi: Discovery Publishing House.

Bhaskara Rao, Digumarti and B.S.V. Dutt, Editors (2003). *Education: Programmes and Policies*. New Delhi: APH Publishing Corporation. ISBN 81-7648-470-9.

Bhaskara Rao, Digumarti and D. Naresh Kumar (2004). *School Teacher Effectiveness*. New Delhi: Discovery Publishing House.

Bhaskara Rao, Digumarti and D. Sridhar (2002). *Job Satisfaction of School Teachers*. New Delhi: Discovery Publishing House. ISBN 81-7141-652-7.

Bhaskara Rao, Digumarti and Digumarti Pushpa Latha (1994). *Achievement in Biology*. New Delhi: Discovery Publishing House. ISBN 81-7141-264-5.

Bhaskara Rao, Digumarti, C. Sridevi and K. Vijaya (1995). *Achievement in Social Studies*. New Delhi: Discovery Publishing House. ISBN 81-7141-281-5.

Bhaskara Rao, Digumarti and Digumarti Pushpa Latha (1995). *Achievement in English*. New Delhi: Discovery Publishing House. ISBN 81-7141-283-1.

Bhaskara Rao, Digumarti and Digumarti Pushpa Latha (1994). *Achievement in Science*. New Delhi: Discovery Publishing House. ISBN 81-7141-280-70.

Bhaskara Rao, Digumarti and Digumarti Pushpa Latha (1995). *Achievement in Mathematics*. New Delhi: Discovery Publishing House. ISBN 81-7141-278-5.

Bhaskara Rao, Digumarti and Digumarti Pushpa Latha, Editors (1998). *International Encyclopaedia of Women*. 5 Volumes. New Delhi: Discovery Publishing House. ISBN 81-7141-410-9.

Vol. 1 *Status of World's Women*. ISBN 81-7141-494-X.

Vol. 2 *Women, Education and Empowerment*. ISBN 81-7141-498-1.

Vol. 3 *Women Challenges and Advancement*. ISBN 81-7141-497-4.

Vol. 4 *Women and Family Health*. ISBN 81-7141-497-4.

Vol. 5 *Women and International Action*. ISBN 81-7141-498-2.

Bhaskara Rao, Digumarti and Digumarti Harshitha (2004). *Adjustment of Adolescents*. New Delhi: Discovery Publishing House.

Bhaskara Rao, Digumarti, Digumarti Pushpa Latha and Digumarti Harshitha, Editors (2001). *Biological Warfare*. New Delhi: Discovery Publishing House. ISBN 81-7141-597-0.

Bhaskara Rao, Digumarti, Digumarti Pushpa Latha and Digumarti Harshitha, Editors (2001). *Women as Educators*. New Delhi: Discovery Publishing House. ISBN 81-7141-602-0.

Bhaskara Rao, Digumarti and Digumarti Harshitha, Editors (2001). *Education in India*. New Delhi: APH Publishing Corporation. ISBN 81-7648-207-2.

Bhaskara Rao, Digumarti, Digumarti Pushpa Latha and Digumarti Harshitha, Editors (2001). *Assessing Learning Achievement*. New Delhi: Discovery Publishing House. ISBN 81-7141-601-2.

Bhaskara Rao, Digumarti, Digumarti Pushpa Latha and Digumarti Harshitha, Editors (2001). *Energy Security*. New Delhi: Discovery Publishing House. ISBN 81-7141-598-9.

Bhaskara Rao, Digumarti, Digumarti Harshitha and K.R.S.S. Rao, Editors (1999). *Advanced Biotechnology*. New Delhi: Discovery Publishing House. ISBN 81-7141-516-4.

Bhaskara Rao, Digumarti and K.R.S. Sambhasiva Rao, Editors (1996). *Current Trends in Indian Education*. New Delhi: Discovery Publishing House. ISBN 81-7141-311-0.

Bhaskara Rao, Digumarti and K. Vijaya (1995). *A Text Book of Evaluation*. Ambala Cantt: The Associated Publishers.

Bhaskara Rao, Digumarti and N.V.M. Mohana Rao (2002). *Problems of Mentally Handicapped Children*. New Delhi: Discovery Publishing House. ISBN 81-7141-645-4.

Bhaskara Rao, Digumarti and S. Chandra Mohan (2002). *Sports Management*. New Delhi: APH Publishing Corporation. ISBN 81-7648-467-9.

Bhaskara Rao, Digumarti and Sk. Johni Basha (2004). *Teachers' Population Education Awareness*. New Delhi: Discovery Publishing House.

Bhaskara Rao, Digumarti, V.V. Rao, V.V. Lakshmi and V.V. Krishna, Editors (1999). *Status and Advancement of Women*. New Delhi: APH Publishing Corporation. ISBN 81-7648-169-6.

Babu, P.C., Author and Digumarti Bhaskara Rao, Editor (2004). *Flowers of Wisdom*. New Delhi: Discovery Publishing House. ISBN 81-7141-695-0.

Babu, P.C., author and Digumarti Bhaskara Rao, Editor (2004). *Worlds of Wisdom*. New Delhi: Discovery Publishing House.

Bhagya Lakshmi, Lingineni, Author and Digumarti Bhaskara Rao, Editor (2000). *Reading and Comprehension*. New Delhi: Discovery Publishing House. ISBN 81-7141-543-1.

Bhuvaneswara Lakshmi, Gadde, Author and Digumarti Bhaskara Rao Editor (2000). *Attitude Towards Science*. New Delhi: Discovery Publishing House. ISBN 81-7141-541-6.

Devraj, T.A.S., Author and Digumarti Bhaskara Rao, Editor (1997). *Trace analysis of Uranium and Thorium*. New Delhi: Discovery Publishing House. ISBN 81-7141-375-7.

Durga Rani, K., Author and Digumarti Bhaskara Rao, Editor (2000). *Educational Aspirations and Scientific Attitudes*. New Delhi: Discovery Publishing House. ISBN 81-7141-555-55.

Dutt, B.S.V. and Digumarti Bhaskara Rao (2001). *Empowering Primary Teachers*. New Delhi: Discovery Publishing House. ISBN 81-7141-615-2.

Ediger, Marlow and Digumarti Bhaskara Rao (1996). *Science Curriculum*. New Delhi: Discovery Publishing House. ISBN 81-7141-321-8.

Ediger, Marlow and Digumarti Bhaskara Rao (2000). *Teaching Mathematics Successfully*. New Delhi: Discovery Publishing House. ISBN 81-7141-552-0.

Ediger, Marlow and Digumarti Bhaskara Rao (2001). *Teaching Science Successfully*. New Delhi: Discovery Publishing House. ISBN 81-7141-600-4.

Ediger, Marlow and Digumarti Bhaskara Rao (2001). *Teaching Social Studies Successfully*. New Delhi: Discovery Publishing House. ISBN 81-7141-596-2.

Ediger, Marlow and Digumarti Bhaskara Rao (2002). *Philosophy and Curriculum*. New Delhi: Discovery Publishing House. ISBN 81-7141-631-4.

Ediger, Marlow and Digumarti Bhaskara Rao (2002). *Improving School Administration*. New Delhi: Discovery Publishing House. ISBN 81-7141-633-0.

Ediger, Marlow and Digumarti Bhaskara Rao (2002). *Elementary Curriculum*. New Delhi: Discovery Publishing House. ISBN 81-7141-658-6.

Ediger, Marlow and Digumarti Bhaskara Rao (2003). *Language Arts Curriculum*. New Delhi: Discovery Publishing House. ISBN 81-7141-657-8.

Ediger, Marlow and Digumarti Bhaskara Rao (2003). *Psychology and Curriculum*. New Delhi: Discovery Publishing House. ISBN 81-7141-691-8.

Ediger, Marlow and Digumarti Bhaskara Rao (2003). *Teaching Language Arts Successfully*. New Delhi: Discovery Publishing House. ISBN 81-7141-678-0.

Ediger, Marlow and Digumarti Bhaskara Rao (2004). *School Curriculum and Administration*. New Delhi: Discovery Publishing House. ISBN 81-7141-709-4.

Ediger, Marlow and Digumarti Bhaskara Rao (2003). *Teaching Mathematics in Elementary Schools*. New Delhi: Discovery Publishing House. ISBN 81-7141-687-X.

Ediger, Marlow and Digumarti Bhaskara Rao (2003). *Teaching Science in Elementary Schools*. New Delhi: Discovery Publishing House. ISBN 81-7141-698-5.

Ediger, Marlow and Digumarti Bhaskara Rao (2003). *School Curriculum and Administration*. New Delhi: Discovery Publishing House. ISBN 81-7141-709-4.

Ediger, Marlow and Digumarti Bhaskara Rao (2003). *Elementary Curriculum Improvement*. New Delhi: Discovery Publishing House. ISBN 81-7141-740-X.

Ediger, Marlow and Digumarti Bhaskara Rao (2004). *Modern Elementary School*. New Delhi: Discovery Publishing House.

Ediger, Marlow and Digumarti Bhaskara Rao (2004): *Relevancy in Elementary Curriculum*. New Delhi: Discovery Publishing House. ISBN 81-7141-751-5.

Ediger, Marlow and Digumarti Bhaskara Rao, (2004). *Teaching Social Studies in Elementary Schools*. New Delhi: Discovery Publishing House.

Ediger, Marlow, B.S.V. Dutt and Digmarti Bhaskara Rao (2003). *Teaching English Successfully*. New Delhi: Discovery Publishing House. ISBN 81-7141-707-8.

Harshitha, Digumarti and Digumarti Bhaskara Rao, Editors (2004). *Educational Innovations*, New Delhi: Discovery Publishing House.

Indira Devi, Author and J. Prasanth Kumar and Digumarti Bhaskara Rao, Editors (2004). *Values in Language Text Books*. New Delhi: Discovery Publishing House.

Jayasree, Kandi, Author and Digumarti Bhaskara Rao, Editor (1999). *Correlates of Socialisation*. New Delhi: Discovery Publishing House. ISBN 81-7141-517-2.

John Babu, Chikati, Author and T.J.R. Prasad, G.M. Madhukar and Digumarti Bhaskara Rao, Editors (1996). *Problem Solving in Mathematics*. New Delhi: APH Publishing Corporation. ISBN 81-7648-273-0.

Lalitha, T., Author and K.S. Prabhakaram, D.S.N. Sastry and Digumarti Bhaskara Rao, Editors (2004). *Educational Philosophic Beliefs*. New Delhi: Discovery Publishing House.

Madhu Bala, Jampala, Author and Digumarti Bhaskara Rao, Editor (2004). *Adjustment Problems of Hearing Impaired*. New Delhi: Discovery Publishing House.

Marja, Talvi and Digumarti Bhaskara Rao, Editors (1996). *Educational Leadership and Social Changes*. New Delhi: Discovery Publishing House. ISBN 81-7141-320-X.

Nirmala, Jyothi M., Author and Digumarti Bhaskara Rao, Editor (2003). *Non-detention System in School Education*. New Delhi: Discovery Publishing House. ISBN 81-7141-654-3.

Prabhakaram, K.S., Author and Digumarti Bhaskara Rao, Editor (1998). *Concept Attainment Model in Mathematics Teaching*. New Delhi: Discovery Publishing House. ISBN 81-7141-424-9.

Prasanth Kumar, J., Author and Digumarti Bhaskara Rao, Editor (1998). *Effectiveness of Distance Education System*. New Delhi: Discovery Publishing House. ISBN 81-7141-437-0.

Prasanth Kumar, J., Author and G. Sundara Rao and Digumarti Bhaskara Rao, Editors (2000). *Open University Student Support Services*. New Delhi: Discovery Publishing House. ISBN 81-7141-550-4.

Ramatulasamma, K., Author and Digumarti Bhaskara Rao, Editor (2002). *Job Satisfaction of Teacher Educators*, New Delhi: Discovery Publishing House. ISBN 81-7141-655-1.

Rama Krishnaiah, D., Author and Digumarti Bhaskara Rao, Editor (1998). *Job Satisfaction of College Teachers*, New Delhi: Discovery Publishing House. ISBN 81-7141-438-9.

Ram Kumar Ratnam, M., Author and Digumarti Bhaskara Rao, Editor (1998). *Dukkha: Suffering in Early Buddhism*. New Delhi: Discovery Publishing House. ISBN 81-7141-653-5.

Rathaiah, Lavu and Digumarti Bhaskara Rao, Editors (1996). *International Innovations in Education*. New Delhi: Discovery Publishing House. ISBN 81-7141-359-5.

Ramesh, Ganta and Digumarti Bhaskara Rao, Editors (1998). *Environmental Education: Problems and Prospects*. New Delhi: Discovery Publishing House. ISBN 81-7141-423-0.

Rathaiah, Lavu and Digumarti Bhaskara Rao (1997). *Achievement Correlates*. New Delhi: Discovery Publishing House. ISBN 81-7141-385-4.

Reddy, Sudhakar Y., Author, and Digumarti Bhaskara Rao, Editor (2003). *Creativity in Adolescents*. New Delhi: Discovery Publishing House. ISBN 81-7141-659-4.

Reddy, M.S., Author and Digumarti Bhaskara Rao, Editor (2004). *Creativity in College Students*. New Delhi: Discovery Publishing House. ISBN 81-7141-697-7.

Radramamba, B., Author and Digumarti Bhaskara Rao, Editor (2003). *Problems of Teaching*. New Delhi: APH Publishing Corporation. ISBN 81-7648-462-8.

Sanjeeva Rao, P.C., Author and Digumarti Bhaskara Rao, Editor (1996). *A Text Book of Geology*. New Delhi: Discovery Publishing House. ISBN 81-7141-313-7.

Satya Narayana V., Author and Digumarti Bhaskara Rao, Editor (2001). *Physical Education, Social Attitudes and Leadership Qualities*. New Delhi: Discovery Publishing House. ISBN 81-7141-593-8.

Srinivasulu Reddy, M., and K.R.S. Sambasiva Rao, Authors and Digumarti Bhaskara Rao, Editor (1999). *A Text Book of Aquaculture*. New Delhi: Discovery Publishing House. ISBN 81-7141-482-6.

Srinivasa Rao, Mandalapu, Author and Digumarti Bhaskara Rao, Editor (2003). *Achievement Motivation and Achievement in Mathematics*. New Delhi: Discovery Publishing House. ISBN 81-7141-674-8.

Vanaja, M. Author and Digumarti Bhaskara Rao, Editor (1999). *Inquiry Training Model*. New Delhi: Discovery Publishing House. ISBN 81-7141-515-6.

Vanaja, M., and N. Sneha Latha and Digumarti Bhaskara Rao (2004). *Student Shyness*. New Delhi: APH Publishing Corporation. ISBN 81-7648-545-4.

Valeri V. Koustiouk, Author and Digumarti Bhaskara Rao, Editor (2002). *A Text Book of Cryogenics*. New Delhi: Discovery Publishing House. ISBN 81-7141-642-X.

Veena Kumari, Balusu and Digumarti Bhaskara Rao (1996). *Operation Black Board*. New Delhi: Discovery Publishing House. ISBN 81-7141-711-X.

Veena Kumari, Balusu, Author and Digumarti Bhaskara Rao, Editor (2000). *Psycho-Social Correlates of Achievement*, New Delhi: Discovery Publishing House. ISBN 81-7141-547-4.

Venkata Rao, P. and Digumarti Bhaskara Rao (1989). *A Text Book of Zoology—Junior Intermediate*. Guntur: Vignan Publishers.

Venkata Rao, P. and Digumarti Bhaskara Rao (1989). *A Text Book of Zoology—Senior Intermediate*. Guntur: Vignan Publishers.

Venugopala Rao, K., Author and Digumarti Bhaskara Rao, Editor (2000). *Teacher Morale in Secondary Schools*. New Delhi: Discovery Publishing House. ISBN 81-7141-551-2.

Vidya, C., Author and Digumarti Bhaskara Rao. Editor (1996). *A Text Book of Nutrition*. New Delhi: Discovery Publishing House. ISBN 81-7141-309-9.

Vidya Bharathi, D., Author and Digumarti Bhaskara Rao, Editor (2000). *Educational Philosophies of Swami Vivekananda and John Dewey*. New Delhi: APH Publishing Corporation. ISBN 81-7648-309-9.

Books in Telugu Language

Bhaskara Rao, Digumarti (1986). *Dhrushya Sravana Bodhanapakaranalu* (Audio Visual Teaching Aids). Guntur: Sri Nagarjuna Publishers.

Bhaskara Rao, Digumarti (1993). *Jeevasashtra Bodhana* (Teaching of Biology). Guntur: Sri Nagarjuna Publishers.

Bhaskara Rao, Digumarti (1995). *Vignanasasthra Bodhana* (Teaching of Science) Guntur: Sri Nagarjuna Publishers.

Bhaskara Rao, Digumarti (1997). *Vidya Manovignana Sashtram* (Educational Psychology). Guntur: Creative Press.

Bhaskara Rao, Digumarti (1998). *DSC Study Material*. Guntur: Sri Nagarjuna Publishers.

Bhaskara Rao, Digumarti (1998). *Upadhyayudu Vidya*. (Teacher and Education). Guntur: Sri Nagarjuna Publishers.

Bhaskara Rao, Digumarti (1998). *Vidya Drukpadalu* (Prespectives of Education). Guntur: Sri Nagarjuna Publishers.

Bhaskara Rao, Digumarti (1999). *EdCET Teaching Aptitude*. Guntur: Sri Nagarjuna Publishers.

Bhaskara Rao, Digumarti (2001). *Bharata Samajamulo Upadyayudu Vidya* (Teacher and Education in Emerging Indian Society). Guntur: Sri Nagarjuna Publishers.

Bhaskara Rao, Digumarti (2001). *Bhoutika Sastra Bodhana Paddathulu* (Methods of Teaching Physical Science). Guntur: Sri Nagarjuna Publishers.

Bhaskara Rao, Digumarti (2001). *Jeeva Sastra Bodhana Padhathulu* (Methods of Teaching Biology). Guntur: Sri Nagarjuna Publishers.

Bhaskara Rao, Digumarti (2001). *Vidya Manovignana Sastram* (Educational Psychology). Guntur: Sri Nagarjuna Publishers.

Bhaskara Rao, Digumarti (2003). *Patsala Yajamanyam / Paripalana* (School Management and Administration). Guntur: Sri Nagarjuna Publishers.

Bhaskara Rao, Digumarti (2004). *Vidya Sanketika Sastram mariyu Computer Vidya* (Educational Technology and Computer Education). Guntur: Sri Nagarjuna Publishers.